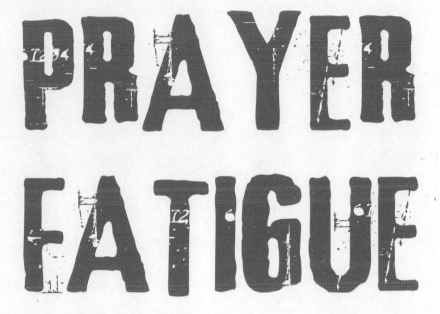

JENNIFER KENNEDY DEAN

10 WAYS TO
REVIVE YOUR PRAYER
LIFE

 NEW HOPE®
PUBLISHERS
Gospel-Centered. Missions-Driven.

BIRMINGHAM, ALABAMA

New Hope® Publishers
P O Box 12065
Birmingham, AL 35202-2065
NewHopeDigital.com
New Hope Publishers is a division of WMU®.

New Hope Publishers serves its authors as they express their views, which may not express the views of the publisher.

Library of Congress Cataloging-in-Publication Data

Dean, Jennifer Kennedy.
 Prayer fatigue : 10 ways to revive your prayer life / Jennifer Kennedy Dean.
 pages cm
 ISBN 978-1-59669-426-2 (sc)
1. Prayer—Christianity. I. Title.
 BV210.3.D436 2015
 248.3'2—dc23
        2014023720

All Scripture quotations, unless otherwise indicated, are taken from the HOLY BIBLE, NEW INTERNATIONAL VERSION®. NIV®. Copyright ©1973, 1978, 2011 by Biblica, Inc.® Used by permission. All rights reserved worldwide.
   Scripture quotations marked AMP are taken from the Amplified® Bible, Copyright © 1954, 1958, 1962, 1964, 1965, 1987 by The Lockman Foundation. Used by permission.
   Scripture quotations marked ESV are from The Holy Bible, English Standard Version, copyright © 2001 by Crossway Bibles, a division of Good News Publishers. Used by permission. All rights reserved.
   Scripture quotations marked The Message are taken from The Message by Eugene H. Peterson. Copyright © 1993, 1994, 1995, 1996, 2000, 2001, 2002. Used by permission of NavPress Publishing Group.
   Scripture quotations marked NASB are taken from the New American Standard Bible®, Copyright © 1960, 1962, 1963, 1968, 1971, 1972, 1973, 1975, 1977, 1995 by The Lockman Foundation. Used by permission.
   Scripture quotations marked NKJV are taken from the New King James Version. Copyright © 1982 by Thomas Nelson, Inc. Used by permission. All rights reserved.
   Scripture quotations marked NLT are taken from the Holy Bible, New Living Translation, copyright © 1996. Used by permission of Tyndale House Publishers, Inc., Wheaton, Illinois. All rights reserved.
   Scripture quotations marked GW are taken from GOD'S WORD®. GOD'S WORD® is a copyrighted work of God's Word to the Nations. Copyright © 1995 by God's Word to the Nations. All rights reserved. Used by permission.

ISBN: 978-1-59669-426-2

N154105 • 0215 • 3M1

OTHER NEW HOPE BOOKS BY
JENNIFER KENNEDY DEAN

Live a Praying Life®: Open Your Life to God's Power and Provision

Live a Praying Life: Open Your Life to God's Power and Provision Bible Study—Tenth Anniversary Edition

Live a Praying Life: Open Your Life to God's Power and Provision DVD Leader Kit—Tenth Anniversary Edition

Live a Praying Life: A Daily Look at God's Power and Provision Journal

Clothed with Power

Altar'd: Experience the Power of Resurrection

Life Unhindered! Five Keys to Walking in Freedom

Secrets Jesus Shared: Kingdom Insights Revealed Through Parables

Secrets Jesus Shared: Kingdom Insights Revealed Through Parables DVD Leader Kit

The Power of Small: Think Small to Live Large

Pursuing the Christ: Prayers for Christmastime

Heart's Cry: Principles of Prayer

Live a Praying Life in Adversity: Why You Keep Praying When You Want to Give Up

Conversations with the Most High: 365 Days in God's Presence

DEDICATION

TO MY PRECIOUS SONS, BEAUTIFUL DAUGHTERS-IN-LAW

Brantley and Caroline Dean

Kennedy and Sara Dean

Stinson and Stephanie Dean

TO MY INCREDIBLE GRANDCHILDREN

Campbell Wayne Dean

Savannah Quin Dean

Audrey Elizabeth Dean

Roger Wayne Dean

And all the others yet to come

CONTENTS

11 ACKNOWLEDGMENTS

13 INTRODUCTION

15 CHALLENGE ONE

Thinking of prayer as one more thing on your already crowded to-do list

33 CHALLENGE TWO

Feeling that your job in prayer is to convince God or to move Him to do your will

57 CHALLENGE THREE

Feeling that God is grading you in prayer and you are passing

75 CHALLENGE FOUR

Trying to follow someone else's pattern for prayer and feeling that you fall short

89 CHALLENGE FIVE

Feeling that in one timeframe—maybe you call it a quiet time—you have to fit in everything included in a predetermined prayer formula

109 CHALLENGE SIX
Being stuck in a prayer rut

127 CHALLENGE SEVEN
Struggling not to let your mind wander

139 CHALLENGE EIGHT
Feeling that prayer is having no effect and is wasted time

159 CHALLENGE NINE
Feeling that you have to perform some kind of spiritual ritual to get God's attention before you can pray

173 CHALLENGE TEN
Feeling so bruised and broken that you don't have the will to participate in anything that requires engagement

189 CONCLUSION

ACKNOWLEDGMENTS

Through these many years of ministry, so many people have enriched my understanding and helped to put the message of a praying life into formats and expressions that have made it accessible.

New Hope® Publishers has to be first on my list. We have grown up together. They published my very first book back in 1990, when I was barely an author and they were barely a publisher. I have continued to publish with them all these years because they are more than a publisher to me. They are a ministry partner.

For most of these years of our partnership, Andrea Mullins was the publisher. Now retired from that position, I just want to publicly acknowledge what her leadership and friendship have meant to me. Her integrity, her vision, her compassion, and her commitment to the message have been indispensable in spreading the teaching about how to live a praying life.

Joyce Dinkins has been my New Hope editor for many years. She is without peer. She also is committed to the integrity of the message, and so does not hesitate to challenge and prod me into the best work I can do.

INTRODUCTION

Have you ever felt disappointed in prayer? Does prayer feel more like a burden than a relief? Does your experience in prayer leave you feeling more worn-out than uplifted? You are not alone.

I have been thinking, studying, teaching, and writing on prayer since I was a young adult. Since the very beginning, I have invited questions from readers and live audiences. This has helped me recognize what concepts need more detail, scriptural evidence, or better illustrations. The questions have challenged me to think through the concepts and examine them from every direction. I'm a question asker by nature, so my whole approach is based on my own questions.

I have taught these concepts in every kind of venue—big, little, urban, rural; geared toward intellectual skeptics or people of straightforward faith; people of all denominations; people of different levels of spiritual maturity or biblical knowledge; people of many different cultures, all over the world. In each of these venues, I have taken live questions.

I think my experience with this one topic qualifies me to say the following: The questions and struggles are consistent. I know that when I invite live questions from my audience, those questions will be the same.

I want to address the challenges of "prayer fatigue" because I think many people experience prayer as a draining and often disappointing activity. The person struggling this way feels that he is the only one who secretly has these questions, and he feels like a failure at prayer. You'll be glad to know that most people feel this way at one time or another. Some stay in that place, probably because they didn't know they could admit what they were feeling and bring their struggles out into the open where they could be examined.

I invite you into this book with an open mind. Let's start from scratch. Let's be uncompromisingly honest about experience and expectations about prayer. Together, let's navigate the twists and turns and find the secret to leaning into prayer as a resting place rather than a struggle.

Each chapter will tackle one reason for prayer fatigue and will include specific adjustments to make in attitude and in practice. Reframing our experiences with prayer in a way that identifies misconceptions and replaces them with truth will cast new light on prayer and its effects. My prayer is that you will find fresh fuel for prayer and new insights into prayer's inner workings. I pray that you will be refreshed and renewed in spirit and will discover the adventure of prayer as God designed it, that prayer will become a force that moves mountains and brings power and provision into your circumstances.

CHALLENGE ONE

**Thinking of prayer as one more thing on
your already crowded to-do list**

PRAYER IS FREEING, NOT RESTRICTIVE

Prayer is not an activity, but a relationship. You live continually in that prayer relationship. It is not something you do, but something you live. Long ago, in the beginning of my prayer exploration, the Lord redefined prayer for me. He said to me, "You don't have a prayer life. You live a praying life."

That recalibrated my understanding of prayer and gave me a different grid through which to view it. Prayer is not about sandwiching words between "Dear God" and "Amen." Prayer is not about getting the words right and putting them in the right order. Prayer is not about adhering to a schedule or a structure. Prayer is freeing, not restrictive. It is simply about living in the flow of the power and provision of God.

If you are in relationship with God through His Son, Jesus, then Jesus has made His home in you. He has taken up residence in you. He is no faraway deity whose attention you hope to garner. He is in you, directing you and transforming you from His position inside you. A comment I often hear goes something like this: "I don't feel like my prayers get past the ceiling." My answer is: "They don't have to go that far!"

This relationship is permanent and always operating. It is not an on-again, off-again relationship. When Jesus moves in, He's all in. Lock, stock, and barrel. We are not always faithful from our side of the relationship, but He is always faithful to us. We are not always fully present to Him, but He is always fully present to us.

My youngest son, Stinson, during his college days, was home for a visit. He and I sat in the same room together. I was thinking about him—was he hungry? Did he need a blanket? I was thinking about his needs. He, on the other hand, was watching a game on television, checking email, texting friends. I said something aloud and he startled, "Oh! I forgot you were here!" Do you see? I was fully present to him, but he was not fully present to me.

Once Jesus is in residence, He is always fully present to you. Your needs and your longings are always before Him. His heart is set on you for good.

Every thought turned in God's direction is prayer. No need for formality. Your words and sentences don't have to align with a set regimen or preset criteria. Your naked heart exposed to the Father's kindness is all it takes.

As you learn to live a praying life, you will become increasingly more aware of the continual interaction between heaven and earth. You will live in the realization that you walk daily in the flow of God's power and provision. An undercurrent of prayer is always active in that person in whom the living, present Jesus dwells.

MULTITASKING

God has created us so that we can always be living praying lives. I don't mean that we are always saying sentences to God. I don't mean that we trade in our responsibilities and relationships for a cloistered, reclusive existence. I mean that God has designed prayer and has fashioned us so that prayer can be always flowing from our hearts to God's. The way He has worked it out is ingenious, His blueprint amazing. I love this little phrase from Colossians 1:16, speaking of Jesus: "All things have been created through him and for him." *For* Him. For His use. He created everything so that everything would be useful for His purposes. He created our brains so that we could live praying lives.

I explained it this way in *Live a Praying Life*:

> Your mind is an amazing creation. It functions efficiently on many levels at once. It is the ultimate multitasking software. At one time you may be driving a car, remembering directions, carrying on a conversation, retaining a grocery list in your memory, observing the time, and on and on and on. There are mental processes going on that you are not even aware of. Consider this: At one of those levels, prayer is always going on. This is true because the Spirit of Christ lives in you and He is always praying. Sometimes, prayer is at the most

conscious and aware level of thought. Other times it is down a level or two. Once I realized that, it became easier and more natural for me to switch back and forth—to bring prayer back to the higher awareness level more often and more spontaneously. The reason is that I don't always feel like I'm starting over. I realize that I'm in a continuous flow of prayer. I didn't stop praying, start doing something else, then start praying all over again. The sweet aroma of prayer is always rising from your innermost being before the throne.

Think of it like this: a certain level of consciousness is always active and available but not always engaged. To illustrate, I'm going to ask you a question you immediately will be able to answer, but until I ask it, you are not consciously thinking of it. Ready? Here goes: what is your Social Security number?

See? There is a level of thinking that is just below the surface of your deliberate thinking. Sometimes prayer is flowing from that level. Sometimes prayer is at that top conscious level. God hears it all just the same.

Think about it. You can be thinking more than one thing at a time. When you are engaged in a conversation, for example, you can be thinking in the back of your mind, "Lord, impart wisdom here." As you are listening to someone's concern, in the back of your mind you can be saying, "I'm lifting this to You, Lord." As you walk out the mundane moments of life, you can be thinking, "You are with me even now. Let me see with Your eyes."

As you feel fear, anxiety, or anger coming on, you can meet these toxic emotions with the overcoming presence of Jesus. Here is how I describe this in my book *Life Unhindered!*

> You can tell that I think in pictures. This is the picture I see with the eyes of my heart when I want to get out of His way and let Him handle something: There I am. Then here comes Jesus. Big, big Jesus. He stands in front of me, but like the cloud of His presence the Israelites knew so well, He is all around me. I am inside Him. Remember how Moses walked into the cloud? "Then Moses entered the cloud as he went on up the mountain" (Exodus 24:18). I might stick my head out and say to the enemy, who is trying his best to get me to follow my flesh's lead, "Take it up with Him."

He is never absent or distracted. Nothing comes to you that is yours to bear or even process on your own. You can always be in conversation with Him in some form, at some level. You will find Him nudging your thoughts in a new direction or reminding you of something that colors the moment. He is alive and living in you. He is active and present-tense and now-speaking. He is not an abstract idea or a set of beliefs. He is real. He is fully present to you all the time.

Like air that surrounds you and presses in on you so that breathing is more natural than not breathing, the very presence of God is your native air. Responding to Him and receiving into your life all He is offering is a natural and instinctive response. Holding Him at a distance requires more work and effort than yielding to Him. He is relentless in His love for you, and He never lets up in His pursuit of you. Prayer is as natural as breathing.

Prayer is not hard or complicated. I repeat, it is not an activity you perform but a relationship in which you live. It is a simple response to His presence. It is your yes to His invitation. It is yielding to His initiative. It is resting your life and your every moment on Him.

PRAYER AS CONDUIT

One of my favorite authors on prayer is Ole Hallesby, and his book *Prayer* is maybe the most influential book on my own understanding of prayer. He says, "Prayer is the conduit through which power from heaven is brought to earth." What is God's intent for prayer? The purpose of prayer is to release the power of God to accomplish the purposes of God. Prayer is not a way that you and I can argue and maneuver God into carrying out our ideas. That is the kind of praying that wears you out. Prayer is just letting the riches and the plans of heaven flow into the circumstances of earth. You don't have to know what to tell God to do. You don't have to have the situation figured out. You can be helpless and hopeless and clueless and still access all the power and provision of God. Your weakest, puniest prayer will access all the power of heaven.

Here is a visual from *Live a Praying Life* to illustrate how prayer, through our intercessor Jesus Christ, becomes the conduit for God's power flowing from heaven to meet our needs on earth.

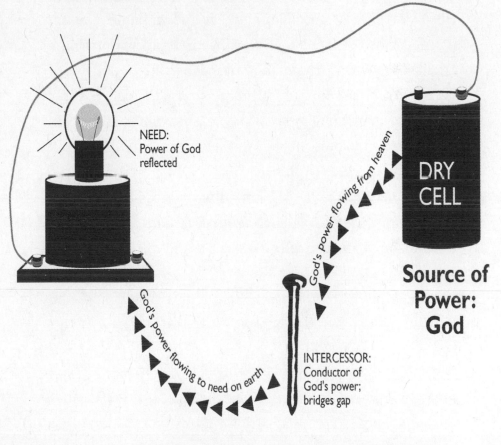

NEED:
Power of God
reflected

God's power flowing from heaven

DRY CELL

Source of
Power:
God

God's power flowing to need on earth

INTERCESSOR:
Conductor of
God's power;
bridges gap

SHORTHAND PRAYING

Do you have people in your life with whom you can communicate with a word, or a touch, or a look? That kind of communication comes with time and intimacy. You can say something in a shorthand style because you've spent time and have shared experience.

My late husband, Wayne, loved Cracker Barrel restaurants. His Alabama roots gave him a love for down-home, country cooking. When our sons were growing up, we spent much time and had many long and memorable conversations and lots of laughs at Cracker Barrel restaurants across the country. It is one of our shared memories of Wayne. From time to time, one of us will text the others: "Just ate at Cracker Barrel." That's all we need to say. We all get it.

My sons have many shorthand ways of communicating with each other. When we're together, I'm often at a loss to understand what just set off gales of laughter, but they all know.

I have two sisters and we share a history. When we are together, we can communicate with a word or a gesture. To us, that word or gesture tells a long story. We read the shorthand as if one of us had told the whole story. It all comes from intimacy and history. The more intimacy, the more shorthand communication.

You will find prayer working the same way. The more you grow in intimacy and the more history you build with God, the simpler your expressions of prayer will become in many ways. You will still have the times of extended conversation and heart-to-heart interaction, but you will also develop a shorthand that will go back and forth throughout the day.

Don't you find that the closer your relationship is with another person, the simpler the communication? I have a prayer team that has been with me for many years, some from the very beginning of my ministry. When I share with them something that has happened, I don't have to go back and explain all the twists and turns over the years that make this event significant because they've been there with me. We have shared history. I can express something to them in a few words that will take long, involved explanation to someone else.

Many times my shorthand prayer is just speaking name of Jesus as someone or something comes to mind. When I greet people with a hug or handshake or touch on the arm, for me it is a shorthand prayer asking the Lord to meet their every need. Sometimes I just say a person's name to the Lord, and He knows all about it.

Another one of my favorite Ole Hallesby quotes is this:

> This power is so rich and so mobile that all we have to do when we pray is to point to the persons or things to which we desire to have this power applied, and He, the Lord of this power, will direct the necessary power to the desired place at once.

Prayer is as simple as pointing. This is not promising a magic solution or an immediate outcome that you are ordering but the immediate application of heaven's power to earth's circumstances. You don't have to be eloquent or long-winded or to get the words right. Just point. In my mind, I point to loved ones all day long. As they come to mind, instead of worrying or trying to figure out how to instruct God to act, in my mind, I just point. Augustine says this eloquently: "Longing desire prayeth always, though the tongue be silent. If thou art ever longing, thou art ever praying."

Does prayer sometimes feel like a burden or responsibility because you think you always have to form sentences and work them into paragraphs for it to count as prayer? Learn the freedom of shorthand prayer.

GO WITH THE FLOW

Once again, prayer is a relationship, not an activity or a performance. A relationship involves connection, involvement, interaction, give-and-take between two parties. It is more than an acquaintance. It entails a mutual commitment, an alliance. It involves a sharing of mind and heart, a unity of intention, a consensus of thought. It requires time spent in each other's company, each focused on the heart of the other.

This praying life—this relationship called prayer—is a relationship like no other because the living, present Jesus, who is the linchpin of this relationship, is not someone outside you; He is inside you. He has direct access to your thoughts, desires, ideas, and hopes. He can speak to you from inside, making direct deposits from His heart to yours. The communication is so intimate that it may feel like a thought that occurred to you.

When another person communicates his thoughts to you from outside, the words he uses may not reach your understanding as the person meant them. How often have you heard someone's words but still misunderstood their meaning? Have you ever had someone respond to your words in a way you did not intend? From the outside, words have to be filtered through many screens: personal interpretations, preset ideas, interpretation of facial expressions or body language. By the time it reaches the understanding, it may bear no resemblance to what the communicator meant.

Let me illustrate how unreliable information from an outside source can be, even if it's true. My niece Hannah was about three years old when Hurricane Andrew hit Florida. Hannah lived in Houston. The weather reports warned that the hurricane might be headed for Houston. My sister Julie said to Hannah, "We have to go to the grocery store and get some food because a hurricane's coming." Hannah asked, "What's a hurricane?" Julie replied, "It's a big storm and it rains and it blows—" Hannah said, "And it eats?" Hannah heard the exact words, but she still missed their meaning.

God has designed this whole relationship of prayer so that He has direct access to your mind and heart. Through the indwelling Jesus, the very heart of God is being reproduced in you. He is speaking to you from inside, bypassing all those screens through which the words might be misconstrued. He is speaking to you in ways that connect to your heart and your personality. Not generalized, generic thoughts but tailored thoughts directly deposited in your heart so that they become part of you.

To me, one of the clearest portrayals of this relationship is found in John 15:5. Jesus expresses it this way: "I am the vine; you are the branches." The life of the vine flows through the branches. The branches are connected to the vine, and what flows through the vine is what flows into the branches. Isn't that a beautiful picture? It depicts a relationship that is vital and flowing. Not something that stops and starts, but something that flows and flows and flows. Living, present-tense relationship.

As acquaintance deepens into relationship, a bond is formed. You have Jesus every moment of every day without intermission. The relationship between you and God, through Jesus, becomes the riverbed in which the days and details of your life flow. This relationship—this riverbed—is what shapes and defines the direction of your life. It gives form and structure to seemingly random happenings and gives them context and meaning.

Think about relationships as you know them. Think of the close, intimate relationships in your life. The relationship is intact and alive even when you are not speaking words. When you are together, you are sharing experience. You are forming deeper bonds. Your relationship is growing just by being together. In your earthly relationships, you are not always together. But with Jesus, there is no moment in which He is not present, no thought to which He is not privy, no emotion you feel of which He does not plumb the depths.

Learn to live in an awareness of this relationship. Determine to be attentive to the presence of Jesus alive in you. Relax in this reality. Let it be your frame of reference. Bring everything—thoughts, words, circumstances, tasks, events, struggles, whatever makes up your life—*everything* into that relationship. Nothing is happening in your life apart from this connection. Whatever it is, Jesus is in it with you. You are not on your own. His power is operating on your behalf. That's what it means to be in relationship with Him. It means you can depend on Him. He never leaves you, never gets distracted, and never dismisses your struggles. Can anything come into your life for which Jesus is not adequate? Can you encounter anything that Jesus is not equipped to handle? Sometimes prayer is just getting out of His way, looking toward Him, and saying, "You handle this, please."

This is the flow of a praying life. Every thought turned toward Him. Are your thoughts always perfect? Not if you're a human being like the rest of us. Can you turn a wrong thought toward Him? Or will He reject you? Here is a secret: Jesus already knows what you're thinking. He invites you to be transparent and honest with Him. No pretense necessary.

He loves you and longs for intimacy with you just as you are. When our wounded thoughts draw us to Him instead of driving us from Him, then we will find that He can heal and redirect our hearts. Don't edit yourself or try to make yourself presentable to Him before you turn your heart to Him. Just turn to Him and let Him heal you and cleanse you and set you free.

Go with the flow of His life in you. Prayer is more than a way to get stuff from God. Prayer is the continual connection between your heart and the heart of the Jesus who flows in you. The inner landscape of your soul is changing. Sometimes with big upheavals but mostly little by little, almost imperceptibly. Like a flowing river changes the landscape, the flowing life of Jesus changes your heart. This interaction between heaven and earth, between His heart and yours, is prayer. Your understanding of prayer changes from something you do to something you live.

REFRAME

Write out the ways your concept of prayer has begun to change.

How is this new understanding of the nature of prayer freeing you from the burden of trying to fit prayer into an overloaded schedule?

Determine that you will be deliberate and purposeful about remaining aware of the living, present Jesus in you. It will be a retraining of your way of processing life, but it will revolutionize your outlook. Right now, how is it changing your perception of events to focus on Jesus' presence and power?

Practice some ways of shorthand prayer. What comes to mind?

CHALLENGE TWO

Feeling that your job in prayer is to convince God or to move Him to do your will

GOD IS DRAWING YOU
TO RECEIVE HIS PROVISION

Prayer is initiated by God. He works in your heart, convincing you and moving you to respond to Him and to open your life to His power and provision. Instead of feeling that you have to work on Him, relax and let Him work in you. God is neither reluctant to respond, nor is He far removed from you. He is immediately accessible and eager to pour out His blessings on you.

When you understand your role in prayer is to influence or change God, it means that you need to be clever enough to decide what God should do and then be articulate and persuasive enough to talk Him into doing it. Quite a responsibility rests on you in that case. Rather than prayer being a release of burden, it becomes an added burden.

Did I make the most convincing case for my point of view? Was I persuasive enough? Did I get through? So many restless thoughts and anxieties accompany this approach to prayer that it wears you out.

> This kind of pray-er sees himself as constantly having to overcome God's objections, or His inertia, or His procrastination. This person feels that God always starts out against him and has to be won over. Prayer of this kind pits the prayer against God. It feels like a battle of wills. —*Live a Praying Life*

You find yourself straining to find the right formula, or the right words to say, or the right order in which to say them. It puts you on a quest to search out the approach to God that will finally get Him to act. Instead, realize that you are being drawn to prayer because God is drawing you to receive His provision. He is pulling you into His activity. He is alerting you that He has answers you lack, and He has resources you do not have.

"And my God will meet all your needs according to the riches of his glory in Christ Jesus" (Philippians 4:19). Look at what Paul said about God here. He will meet *all* your needs. Every need, with no exclusions of any kind of need. Every kind of need. He *will* meet—He will fulfill, He will take care of, He will supply—every need. *He* will. He Himself takes responsibility for every single need.

Now, look at the storehouse from which the supply will come: "the riches of his glory." If you were to come to me and ask me to meet a need for you, I would do the best I could, but I would be restricted by the supply I had available. I might say, "I'll meet your need in accordance with my available riches." My available riches would draw the boundary for my generosity. I could only be as generous as my available supply allowed. God has no boundaries to His ability and willingness to meet your need. The riches of His glory are boundless and fathomless and inexhaustible. His riches are warehoused in Christ Jesus, whom He has given to indwell you. Jesus is actively distributing the riches of glory into the lives of believers in response to prayer. Everything God has is on deposit in Christ, and Christ is actively working in you and through you.

GOD WANTS TO ANSWER PRAYER

It is not hard to get God to answer prayer. Prayer is His idea. God thought up prayer, not us. God put prayer into the equation as the means by which my need could find His supply. E. Stanley Jones says it this way in *Abundant Living*, "Prayer is . . . the opening of a channel from your emptiness into God's fullness."

God established prayer as the conduit through which His power and provision flow out of heaven and into the circumstances of earth. Jesus prayed: "Let Your will that has been done in heaven, now be done on earth" (Matthew 6:10; author's paraphrase). Jesus understood prayer to be the bridge between heaven and earth, accessing heaven's provision for earth's needs.

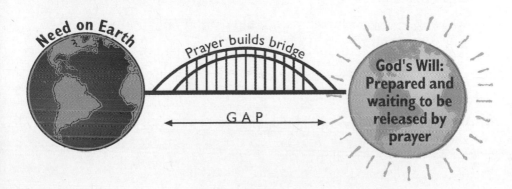

God put prayer into the eternal equation because He wants His provision and His power to be available for all of earth's circumstances. He desires for us to know from our experience that His intervening power can change the course events are taking on their own. He wants us to see His activity in our daily lives so that we will be bound by our hearts to Him and develop confidence in His ability to overcome every obstacle and overpower every hindrance. When we see His direct action in response to prayer, our faith grows and our confidence in Him increases. We learn to live at peace, knowing that His power is flowing through prayer into our circumstances.

Maybe you would describe your prayer experience this way: "I prayed and prayed, but the obstacle did not move." Let me suggest this to consider. Maybe the thing you saw as an obstacle to be removed God knew would protect you from moving forward in a way that looked right in the moment but would prove later to be a mistake. Maybe you wore yourself out praying, only to be disappointed in the end. Maybe that one experience convinced you that prayer doesn't work and caused you to give up in defeat. Remember, prayer is not a way to get God to do what you think should be done. Rather, it is the way to conduct the power and wisdom of God into the circumstances of earth. If the result of prayer is that an obstacle stays stubbornly in place, or a door stays closed, then that is protection. A closed door is as much a yes from God as an open door.

Looking back on my history with God, I can see in retrospect what was not evident in the moment. What I thought of at the time as a setback or defeat turned out to be a safeguard. What looked like a failure turned out to be the event that moved me into the direction where God's design for my life gained traction.

When prayer did not have the result you wanted, remember that you don't know all that God knows. To be able to know prayer as restful, you have to be confident of the God to whom your prayers are directed. You have to have full assurance that He is all-wise, that He knows the end from the beginning, that He is only loving, that He has plans for you that are for your good, that He is working strategically toward with an end in mind.

Examine what the Scripture tells us about who God is and why He is completely trustworthy.

All Wise, Understanding All Things

"To God belong wisdom and power; counsel and understanding are his" (Job 12:13).

"Do you not know? Have you not heard? The Lord is the everlasting God, the Creator of the ends of the earth. He will not grow tired or weary, and his understanding no one can fathom" (Isaiah 40:28).

"Great is our Lord and mighty in power; his understanding has no limit" (Psalm 147:5).

"Oh, the depth of the riches of the wisdom and knowledge of God! How unsearchable his judgments, and his paths beyond tracing out! 'Who has known the mind of the Lord? Or who has been his counselor?'" (Romans 11:33–34).

The word *wisdom* might be summed up as technical know-how. Wisdom is based on understanding. Because God can see to the very heart of any matter (understanding), He knows how to bring about the absolutely right conclusion to any matter (wisdom). A. W. Tozer defines wisdom in *The Knowledge of the Holy*: "Wisdom, among other things, is the ability to devise perfect ends and to achieve those ends by the most perfect means. It sees the end from the beginning, so there can be no need to guess or conjecture. Wisdom sees everything in focus, each in proper relation to all, and is thus able to work toward predestined goals with flawless precision."

All-Knowing, Knowing the End from the Beginning

"I make known the end from the beginning, from ancient times, what is still to come. I say, 'My purpose will stand, and I will do all that I please'" (Isaiah 46:10).

"Nothing in all creation is hidden from God's sight. Everything is uncovered and laid bare before the eyes of him to whom we must give account" (Hebrews 4:13).

If God did not know the end from the beginning, then how could He make promises about the future? If He were making things up as He goes, how could He ask us to put confidence in His plan? If His purposes were not certain to stand when the dust settles, then on what basis could we rest in Him? The Scripture declares over and over that He is not at a loss but instead that He knows and holds the future.

To illustrate the detailed nature of His knowledge, the Scripture uses descriptions such as: He knows the number of hairs on your head (Matthew 10:30); He knows when a sparrow falls from the sky (10:29); He knows each star and calls them each by name (Psalm 147:4); He knows the thoughts and intentions of the heart (Hebrews 4:12); He knows each step we take (Proverbs 20:24); and He knows when we lie down or when we rise up (Psalm 139:2). He knows every detail; He is a micromanager. When He works in your life, His work is based on detailed knowledge of every aspect of the situation. He knows you better than you know yourself. He knows past, present, and future. He knows the details of every situation that intersects with yours. He is *all*-knowing.

Only Loving

"You are good, and what you do is good" (Psalm 119:68).

"For the Lord is good and his love endures forever; his faithfulness continues through all generations" (Psalm 100:5).

"He does not treat us as our sins deserve or repay us according to our iniquities. For as high as the heavens are above the earth, so great is his love for those who fear him" (Psalm 103:10–11).

"What can we say about all of this? If God is for us, who can be against us? God didn't spare his own Son but handed him over [to death] for all of us. So he will also give us everything along with him. Who will accuse those whom God has chosen? God has approved of them. Who will condemn them? Christ has died, and more importantly, he was brought back to life. Christ has the highest position in heaven. Christ also intercedes for us. What will separate us from the love Christ has for us? Can trouble, distress, persecution, hunger, nakedness, danger, or violent death separate us from his love? . . . The one who loves us gives us

an overwhelming victory in all these difficulties.
I am convinced that nothing can ever separate
us from God's love which Christ Jesus our Lord
shows us. We can't be separated by death or life,
by angels or rulers, by anything in the present or
anything in the future, by forces or powers in the
world above or in the world below, or by anything
else in creation" (Romans 8:31–35, 37–39 GW).

He has no purpose in His heart toward you other than love. His plans for you are formed out of pure, unalloyed love for you. Nothing else motivates His actions in your life. You can count on His unwavering, staunch, unflagging love for you. In Romans 8:31–39, Paul takes time to list every kind of difficulty and challenge we may ever encounter and declares that nothing will separate us from His love. That's how tenacious His love is. It holds on. Because of this astounding love, we will always come out the victor. His great love will see to it.

He doesn't coddle you, but He protects and defends you. He doesn't indulge you, but He supplies you with His abundance. He doesn't preclude difficulties in your life, but He filters them and screens them so that only that which will enrich you enters your experience. His love is dependable and absolutely trustworthy.

He Is Working Strategically, and His Plans Are for Your Good

> *"'For I know the plans I have for you,' declares the Lord, 'plans to prosper you and not to harm you, plans to give you hope and a future'"* (Jeremiah 29:11).

> *"Many, Lord my God, are the wonders you have done, the things you planned for us. None can compare with you; were I to speak and tell of your deeds, they would be too many to declare"* (Psalm 40:5).

> *"For you created my inmost being; you knit me together in my mother's womb. I praise you because I am fearfully and wonderfully made; your works are wonderful, I know that full well. My frame was not hidden from you when I was made in the secret place, when I was woven together in the depths of the earth. Your eyes saw my unformed body; all the days ordained for me were written in your book before one of them came to be"* (Psalm 139:13–16).

You can trust that God is working in your life according to a strategy that He thought through and laid out before you were born. Nothing He does is aimless or indiscriminate.

Part A will fit into part B. All the disparate pieces will coalesce into a whole. Nothing is wasted or out of place. It all fits. From His all-knowing, all-wise, perfectly loving perspective, He is working all things out, weaving them together toward an end that is for your good (Romans 8:28).

You do not need to convince Him to want to answer prayer. God wants to answer prayer. God does answer prayer.

I DON'T KNOW WHAT TO PRAY

Have you ever said something like this: "I just don't know how to pray about this"? Would you agree that the underlying meaning is: "I just don't know what to tell God to do" or "I'm not sure what instructions to give God"?

When you feel that your role is to give God specific instructions to follow, then you will often be at a loss. Or, you will find yourself disappointed that God did not follow the instructions you gave Him.

A praying life is not about determining the best outcome and then influencing God to agree with your assessment. A praying life is not about belief in an outcome, but rather it is about faith in God. Here is where the solid bedrock basis of prayer is found—God. The nature of God. The reality of God. The sovereign power of God. The love of God.

God does not pledge Himself to perform at your command. He does not promise to carry out your ideas. He does not commit Himself to the best thing you can think of. Instead,

He promises to do more than you can ask or even imagine. The Apostle Paul says it like this: "Now all glory to God, who is able, through his mighty power at work within us, to accomplish infinitely more than we might ask or think" (Ephesians 3:20 NLT).

Here's the good news about the kind of prayer that accesses all the power of heaven: You don't have to give God the answer; you just need to bring Him the need. Hand the need over to Him and let Him handle everything. Every detail, every situation, every step of the process is His to work out. He is willing and even eager to take your problem and make it His responsibility. Not only does He work everything out with your good in mind, but He uses the very struggles and challenges that confront you to enrich you and bring you into the destiny and purpose for which you were created. He wastes nothing.

"And we know that in all things God works for the good of those who love him, who have been called according to his purpose" (Romans 8:28).

Do you wonder if you have been called according to His purpose? Right now embrace this: you have been called. You exist because He has a purpose for your existence. Revelation 4:11 (*The Message*) says, "Worthy, O Master! Yes, our God! Take the glory! the honor! the power! You created it all; It was created because you wanted it."

Everything God created—including you—exists because He wants it to exist. He has a purpose for its existence. God did not create a purpose for you. Rather, He created you for a purpose. You have a purpose that fits you as if tailor-made. God is using everything in your life to usher you into the life that suits you. Your calling and God's design are one and the same. Let Him use everything in your life to move you forward. Trust that all things in your life are being worked together for your good. Something good is being accomplished that can't come about any other way. Every difficulty or challenge is shaping and strengthening you. No pain, no gain.

Open your life to His work through prayer. Let God manage the details—the what, when, where, how. Lean in to His purpose. You will find that His purpose for you is the life that will bring you all the peace, joy, and fulfillment that you are seeking. It all waits for you in Him.

WHAT ABOUT PRAYING SPECIFICALLY?

Some of you are thinking: "I've always heard that specific prayers get specific answers, and that we should pray specifically so God will know what we truly want."

It depends on what you mean by praying specifically. If you mean to give God specifics about what He should do and when He should do it, then I suspect that you have had some disappointing experiences when it comes to praying specifically. However, if you mean to bring every detail of your circumstance or concern to Him for Him to release His power and provision into, then you have seen something of the exciting adventure that prayer can be.

Let's think this through. Is God ever confused about your specific desires, and does that throw off the way He answers? First, God knows your true desires better than you do. He has imparted to you the desires that are in your heart. He originates them. He gives you your desires. "Take delight in the Lord, and he will give you the desires of your heart" (Psalm 37:4). The words translated "give" are Hebrew words meaning to give, to cause, to place, to produce, to appoint. He appoints and places the true desires of your heart.

Pay attention to what the Scripture says here: "It is God who works in you to will and to act in order to fulfill his good purpose" (Philippians 2:13). Who is doing the work? God is. Where is the epicenter of God's work? In you. What does His expended energy (work) from within you produce? Both the desire to fulfill His purpose and the ability to fulfill His purpose.

God's work in your life is creating your desires. Shaping your inclinations. Always refining your longings. The true desires of your heart are placed by God and are the echo of His desires for you.

He hears at a level deeper than our words. He is more than a lip reader. He is a heart reader. Sometimes, what we are asking for is not our true desire, but rather it is what we think would meet our true desire. We often mistake the desires of the moment for the desire of our hearts.

A friend's son was incarcerated. She had prayed and prayed that he would not be sentenced to prison, but in her view, her prayers were not answered. She came to me to try to understand how she might have prayed more effectively so that God would have done as she had begged him to do. As we discussed, I helped her identify her true desire—that her son would return to the Lord and live fully in that relationship. I encouraged her to keep that the focus of her praying. She prayed specifically for him: for the right friends and relationships to find him; for each day to be filled with evidence of God's love for him; for mealtimes and work assignments and random conversations and recreation times and bunk mates. Specifically laying every minute of his day at God's feet, but not giving God specific instructions to follow. Specific praying. In prison, he joined a Bible study and there met the Lord at a deep place. He continued to be discipled throughout his prison experience and years after his release is a living testimony of God's redemption. When she got a no to the desire of the moment, she got a yes to the desire of her heart.

Second, God has committed Himself to the desire of your heart. He has shaped the desire of you heart. He knows the deepest parts of the desire or your heart. He will not be distracted from the desire of your heart.

Third, God knows what we do not. He knows the future; He knows the past; He knows all the details along the way. If you knew right now as God knows, you would make the same decisions He makes.

You don't have to give God specific instructions so that He will know what you truly want. We have whims. God has plans. If there were some kind of code we could crack that would enable us to get God to follow our directions, what kind of mess would we make? We would make all our plans based on what seems best to us with our limited view and finite understanding. Our small and selfish goals would prove to be unfulfilling. We would be left empty. Pacified for the moment, but never satisfied for the long term.

Through prayer, bring God into every detail and release His power into the minutiae. Pray specifically, but don't try to give specific orders.

A PRAYER LIST PRAYER LIFE

At some point in my own journey to understand prayer, I realized that I was living what I now call a "prayer list prayer life." I wrote about this revelation and change in perspective in *Live a Praying Life* as follows.

> If God did what was on my list, He answered. If He didn't do what was on my list, He didn't answer, or He said no. And this became the measure of prayer's effectiveness. A "prayer list prayer life" begins to build a distorted understanding of prayer. According to the prayer list, sometimes God says yes and sometimes God says no. Since the praying person would have no way of knowing whether this is a time when God will say yes, or this is a time when God will say no, it becomes very hard to pray

boldly and confidently. As you are learning to live a praying life, prayer takes on a much broader definition than "saying prayers." Much of what prayer is accomplishing cannot be condensed to a list. Many times the direct answers to petitions are the least important aspect of what the prayer accomplished. I believe that as you progress and mature into a praying life, your testimony of prayer's effectiveness will be that the mercies of God unfold at every turn. You walk in answered prayer. . . . Prayer lists are effective if they are in the context of a praying life. Use your prayer list like this: Write down the concern or the need and date it. The date is the day you surrendered it to God for His purposes, His ways, and His timing. Now, don't watch to see if God answers; watch to see how God answers. You will find that He answers progressively. He puts together pieces, each one building on the other. Record things as you go along and watch with amazement as God pieces things together for an outcome that is more than you could think or imagine.

Author Daniel Henderson writes about his own journey out of a request-based prayer life into a worship-based prayer experience in his book *Transforming Prayer*. He makes the point that experiencing prayer as a long list of things God should perform left him empty and unsatisfied with prayer.

But as he learned that prayer's foundation is God's face rather than God's hand, he began what has been a lifetime of passion for prayer.

> Of course, our prayer requests are a vital part of prayer. The Bible is clear about the need to ask God for things and share our burdens with one another. The rut occurs when we allow requests to serve as the foundation of our praying: focusing on our problems rather than actually engaging with God in a multifaceted biblical prayer experience. Clearly, the request-based approach just did not work for me. I have learned that it has not worked for many seeking Christians. This dissatisfaction led me to a growing and life-changing understanding of what I call worship-based prayer. . . . Worship-based prayer seeks the face of God before the hand of God. God's face is the essence of who He is. God's hand is the blessing of what He does. God's face represents His person and presence. God's hand expresses His provision for needs in our lives. I have learned that if all we ever do is seek God's hand, we may miss His face; but if we seek His face, He will be glad to open His hand and satisfy the deepest desires of our hearts.

TO SUM UP

1. Bring God your every request and need and desire, but don't make your list the foundation of your prayer or the measure of your prayer.

2. Use your list to record God's work, not to measure how His activity matched your demands and expectations.

3. Know that each situation, need, and desire that you hand over to God is receiving His full attention. His power and His plan are operating in the midst of every prayer request. You don't have to beg or cajole or influence. Just release.

4. Let your heart come to rest on the presence and the being of God. Let your heart-to-heart interaction with Him form the bedrock of your praying life.

CAST YOUR CARES

"Cast your cares on the Lord and he will sustain you; he will never let the righteous be shaken" *(Psalm 55:22).*

Do you see the invitation here? The Lord invites you to cast your cares away and let them land on Him. He will take them on His own shoulders and carry the weight of them. Your burdens can be transferred from you to Him. You don't have to make a moving speech about them, or persuasively argue the need, or make a convincing case. Just cast them away and let them land on Him. Let Him deal with them. Eugene Peterson translates the same verse this way: "Pile your troubles on God's shoulders—he'll carry your load, he'll help you out" (*The Message*).

Name each burden as you cast it away to Him and let that be your prayer list. Write it down and date it if you want. Let it stand as the record of when you cast that particular burden on the Lord. Then stand back and watch Him work.

When I look back through journals from years back, I see how God has worked in situations in ways I never would have had the imagination to think up. I read entries and remember how things felt in that moment. I often think, *If I could go back and tell my younger self something, I'd tell her there was never anything to worry about.* I see the time and emotion I used up. I realize that the agonizing came out of the fact that I had no control. I couldn't create or force the resolution. But I couldn't just settle into that. Oh, younger Jennifer. If only you knew by experience what you believed with all your heart. Younger Jennifer believed all the truth about God and His ways, but she didn't have a good enough track record yet. Have you ever heard someone say, "I have it in my head, but I can't get it into my heart"? I think the process is just the opposite. There are truths my heart fully embraces, but I can't get them to my head where I make decisions and choose my approach. Time and experience form the road by which heart-held truth travels into the mind where choices are cemented. God is patient. Each experience with the prayer of relinquishment—casting cares on Him—is moving truth into position.

Be grateful for each opportunity to learn by experience what it's like to cast your cares on Him. Be as patient with yourself as God is with you. Let your prayer list be the record of how God worked over time through unexpected twists and turns. I think God loves to use the knight's move. In chess, all the other pieces move in straight directions—forward, backward, horizontal—but straight. The knight, though, moves two squares horizontally and one square vertically, or two squares vertically and one square horizontally. The knight's move appears to be taking the knight in one direction but lands it in a different place altogether. The knight is also the only chess piece that can jump over other pieces, so no piece of either side can stand between the knight and its destination. God often uses the knight's move. Your prayer list, viewed in retrospect, will demonstrate that God doesn't usually take the straight line. He has moves you have never thought of.

What you learn from building history with God is that what was true in the past is true in the moment. God calls us to remember, because in remembering the past we can more readily stand firm in the present.

"Remember the wonders he has done, his miracles, and the judgments he pronounced" (Psalm 105:5).

"I remember the days of long ago; I meditate on all your works and consider what your hands have done" (Psalm 143:5).

REFRAME

Have you been living a prayer list prayer life? If so, write out your list. Beside each item, write a word or phrase that means something to you, like *yours*, or *surrendered*, or *I trust You*.

REFOCUS

Be deliberate about keeping your focus on God Himself and His great love for you and His power to act and His wisdom to know every detail. Retrain yourself to live in a surrendered frame of mind—trusting and confident—rather than anxiously trying to make your requests in such a way that God will do as you have prescribed.

CHALLENGE THREE

Feeling that God is grading you in prayer and you are barely passing

YOU DON'T HAVE TO GET THE WORDS RIGHT

God is not criticizing you and scolding you. He is not withholding His blessings from you because you did not say your prayer correctly. The Holy Spirit has perfected your expression of prayer in the spiritual realm, and God is responding to the cry of your heart, not the cry of your lips.

Because prayer is so powerful and because it is designed by God as the conduit through which heaven's power flows into earth's circumstances, we have an enemy in the spiritual realm whose goal is to hinder prayer in every possible way. He understands how powerful prayer is, and he wants to keep you from it.

"Keep a cool head. Stay alert. The Devil is poised to pounce, and would like nothing better than to catch you napping" (1 Peter 5:8 *The Message*).

The phrase *catch you napping* is a metaphor, of course. It means to be passive and distracted from the main thing. But see Jesus' reaction when He found His disciples literally napping rather than praying.

> When he came back to his disciples, he found
> them sound asleep. He said to Peter, "Can't you
> stick it out with me a single hour? Stay alert; be
> in prayer so you don't wander into temptation

without even knowing you're in danger. There is a part of you that is eager, ready for anything in God. But there's another part that's as lazy as an old dog sleeping by the fire. (Matthew 26:40–41 The Message)

In the Garden of Gethsemane, as Jesus faced His crucifixion, He had asked His disciples to "keep watch with me" (Matthew 26:40) as He prayed. When He found them sleeping and expressed His dismay, He said, "Watch and pray" (Matthew 26:41 ESV). This makes it clear that the watch or the vigil was to be prayer.

Let's put these thoughts together. Jesus says that being alert in prayer will keep us from wandering heedlessly into temptation. Paul says that your enemy in the spiritual realm is seeking to pounce, and so he wants to find you vulnerable and distracted. What keeps you watchful and vigilant—wise to the enemy's schemes? Living in a prayerful state of mind—living a praying life.

Your enemy wants to keep you from praying. It is his goal and the endpoint of his every scheme. Your prayer is his downfall so he works diligently against it. His strategy is to lie to you about prayer and about God. It has always been his strategy. Here's how Jesus describes him: "When he lies, he speaks his native language, for he is a liar and the father of lies" (John 8:44). One of his best lies to keep you from praying is that you're not good at it and God is always disappointed in the quality of your prayers.

Maybe one or several of these accusations are what seem true to you. *You're too selfish. You don't deserve anything from God. You don't have enough faith. You're too sinful. You always say your prayers wrong. You don't know how to pray.*

Any of those ring true for you? Lies, every one. Yet, if not recognized as lies, each can effectively discourage you from praying. So let's dismantle the lies and find the very truth they are meant to disguise. Each of his lies has a specific truth it pinpoints. Where there is a lie from the enemy, there is a truth it intends to disguise.

GOD'S DESIGN FOR PRAYER

We've already addressed the fact that God is the one who designed prayer and put prayer into the equation as the force that would move His power and provision from heaven to earth. Why did He set things up so that He included us in His plans for intervening in the circumstances of earth? Why didn't He just keep things simple by going around us and doing His work without our cooperation—without engaging us through prayer?

It astounds me when I think about how to answer this because it brings out one of the unexpected facets of the salvation God arranged for us. He could have composed a plan for salvation that saved us from the penalty of our sins and brought us into heaven but still kept us at arm's length. Instead, He has provided a salvation that includes intimacy with Him from the moment we believe and accept His gift.

He wants dynamic, interactive relationship with us. He does not want us to be puppets on His string or game pieces on His board. He wants us to be organically connected to His heart and to be fully engaged in His activity. He wants us to be aware of His work and in touch with His power. He invites us to live in sync with His Spirit. "Since we live by the Spirit, let us keep in step with the Spirit" (Galatians 5:25). He wants us to live with our spiritual antennae attuned to His voice. His design for prayer requires us to be tuned in to His frequency, and it requires Him to be present and available to us.

Your heart was made for Him. Your heart longs for Him. All the things we think we want are just cheap substitutes for His presence. Everything He has created us to crave is revealed in the promise of His presence. Every desire our hearts hold is satisfied in His presence. In His presence we find joy and gladness (see Psalm 21:6). Let the presence of the Lord be your daily destination. It doesn't matter where you are or what you're doing, you can be in the presence of God. He is seeking you out. He is drawing you to Himself. You only need to respond. He is right there inside you, wooing you and inviting you to turn away from yourself and toward Him. Calling us to interactive love. Calling us to prayer.

God calls us into prayer by planting a desire in our hearts, or by allowing a need to surface in our lives, or by calling our attention to a plight that requires His intervening power. It creates an inclination to turn to God in prayer. From our side, it feels like our idea to pray. If we could see it from heaven's viewpoint, we would realize that we feel inclined and moved to pray because God is drawing us into prayer.

Sometimes we may feel that we are imposing on God or that we are audacious to think God might be bothered by our little lives, but the reality is that God is coaxing us. He wants us to live in interaction with Him. "In prayer and its answer the interchange of love between the Father and His child takes place" (Andrew Murray, *With Christ in the School of Prayer*).

Every time you feel a pull toward God or an inclination to pray, you are responding to God's invitation to come to Him. You are experiencing just a hint of the love He has for you that makes Him desire your presence. You are being drawn into the orbit of His activity to be a participant and not an observer. Far from imposing on Him, you are instead delighting Him by yielding to His longing for relationship with you.

Think of it. The Creator and Sustainer of the universe devised a plan that would require interaction between heaven and earth. He constructed a device for accessing His riches that made our mutual participation essential to the process. For the plan to work, we need to be desperately dependent on the present voice of God to hear His call, and He needs to be vigilantly accessible to us—responding even to our sighs and groans as if they were perfectly formed sentences.

"All my longings lie open before you, LORD; my sighing is not hidden from you" (Psalm 38:9).

"Give ear to my words, O LORD, Consider my groaning" (Psalm 5:1).

"Before a word is on my tongue you, LORD, know it completely" (Psalm 139:4).

His ear is always open to what rises from your heart, whatever form it takes. He is pulling you into His activity and reproducing His heart in you. He is forming the desires in your heart that your lips speak as prayer. In prayer, you are responding to Him.

GETTING IT RIGHT

God is not grading you. Whatever form your words take, God is hearing beyond your lips to your heart. Your most stumbling attempts at prayer are heard in heaven's throne room as if you had perfectly articulated them. I illustrate this concept in *Power in the Name of Jesus* as follows:

> My oldest son, Brantley, made up his own lan-
> guage as a toddler. He really didn't have to learn
> to talk like the rest of us and use our mundane
> words because his words accomplished just what
> he wanted. Because I so intently observed him,

I always knew what he meant. For example, he had a phrase for "music." He called it something like "mawk mawk." He would say that phrase, and to everyone else's ears it sounded like gibberish, but I knew exactly what it meant. I responded to it as if he had said, "Dearest Mother, would you mind turning on some music?" Even though the sounds he formed fell far short of the true words, they achieved the same end as a perfectly formed sentence would have achieved for him. So it is when you and I speak a ragged and imperfect version of the Name. Heaven responds to it as if it had been spoken flawlessly, in all its glory."

God hears your prayers—the cries of your heart—even before you connect words to them. While the need and desires are so deep in you that they haven't even reached a level of awareness in which you have sentences to express them in, God is already hearing and responding.

Psalm 139:4 says, "Before a word is on my tongue you know it completely, O LORD." Before a need or desire has reached a level of conscious understanding at which you can put it into words—while it is still unformed and raw—God already knows it fully. In Romans 8:26–27, we read, "The Spirit himself intercedes for us through wordless groans. And he who searches our hearts knows the mind of the Spirit, because the Spirit intercedes for God's people in accordance with the will of God." When a desire is nothing but an inarticulate groan— before you can form it into sentences—the Spirit of God is already speaking it with perfect clarity. By the time you begin to speak your need or desire in prayer, you are simply joining into a flow of prayer that is already in progress. "Before they call I will answer; while they are still speaking I will hear" (Isaiah 65:24).

You don't have to get the words right. As you mature in prayer and continue living a praying life, more often the words you express in prayer will match the desires God has placed in your heart, but your words will never be the measure of how effectively you prayed. The minute you turn toward the Father, all of heaven is at the ready.

> To pray is nothing more involved than to let Jesus into our needs. To pray is to give Jesus permission to employ His powers in the alleviation of our distress. To pray is to let Jesus glorify His name in the midst of our needs. The results of prayer are, therefore, not dependent upon the powers of the one who prays. Our intense will, our fervent emotions, or our clear comprehension of what we are praying for are not the reasons why our prayers will be heard and

answered. Nay, God be praised, the results of prayer are not dependent upon these things! To pray is nothing more involved than to open the door, giving Jesus access to our needs and permitting Him to exercise His own power in dealing with them.

So simple. No fuss. Answers to prayer are not rewards for getting prayer right. When your heart is turned Godward, prayer is happening. That's all it takes.

I DON'T DESERVE GOD'S GOODNESS

No matter how sophisticated your prayer theology might become, it is possible that this thought trips you up every time. Because it is true. We don't deserve God's goodness. That statement on its own is true. But it works itself into a lie when we believe that God's goodness is a reward that we may earn or deserve.

Jesus has earned God's goodness for us. From the moment we receive Him as our personal Savior, we are becoming on the outside—in the reality of daily living—what we have been made on the inside. It is a progression that starts at our new birth and goes on until our physical death, but it is always moving forward. Sometimes the progress is accelerated, and other times it moves so slowly it seems to be stalled. But righteousness is always gaining ground. We are always, as

Athanasius of Alexandria stated, "becoming by grace what God is by nature" (*De Incarnatione*, I).

In a praying life, God is using every situation, every moment in our lives, to move us forward in righteousness. His goal is not that we get to the place where we deserve His goodness because that will never happen. His goal is that we progress in the righteousness for which we were designed. At the moment of our salvation, Jesus came to live in us and from that point forward is doing the work only He can do.

First, He has made you worthy in God's eyes by paying in full for your every sin and assigning His own righteousness to you as if it were yours. Second, He undertakes to do in you the work that you cannot accomplish on your own. Because of Jesus, you stand before God unashamed and worthy. God loves you as if you were Jesus. In his letter to the Romans, Paul says this: "He who did not spare his own Son, but gave him up for us all—how will he not also, along with him, graciously give us all things?" (Romans 8:32). You are worth everything to God. He did not hold back even His most cherished, most prized, most adored Son Jesus to win you and bring you into relationship with Him. Do you really think now that He is standing back and criticizing you and devaluing you? You are utterly precious to Him, warts and all. Prayer is what He has established to keep you close to His heart, not to put you under His microscope and look for flaws.

The Scripture tells us that we are clothed with Christ.

"Rather, clothe yourselves with the Lord Jesus Christ, and do not think about how to gratify the desires of the flesh" (Romans 13:14).

"All of you who were baptized into Christ have clothed yourselves with Christ" (Galatians 3:27).

Not only does Jesus fill you on the inside, but He covers you on the outside. The reason we can stand unashamed in God's presence is because we are clothed in Christ. Contrast that with our condition apart from Christ. No matter how many good deeds we perform, "all our righteous acts are like filthy rags" (Isaiah 64:6). Our old past attempts to be good enough, which ended in failure, are replaced by the very presence of Christ in our lives. We are washed clean, made spotless, and robed in the righteousness of Jesus. You have been made deserving.

NOT ENOUGH FAITH

Faith is not something you work up and then present to God in return for favors. Neither is it making yourself believe in an outcome you want to see. Faith is simply entrusting yourself fully to the faithfulness of God.

Scripture goes to great lengths to show us that a little faith—just a speck of faith—is all it takes to access all the power of God.

"I tell you the truth, if you have faith as small as a mustard seed, you can say to this mountain, 'Move from here to there' and it will move. Nothing will be impossible for you" (Matthew 17:20).

I'm fascinated by this story told in the gospels because it shows what just a little faith accomplishes.

> *Then he got into the boat and his disciples fol-lowed him. Suddenly a furious storm came up on the lake, so that the waves swept over the boat. But Jesus was sleeping. The disciples went and woke him, saying, "Lord, save us! We're going to drown!"*
>
> *He replied, "You of little faith, why are you so afraid?" Then he got up and rebuked the winds and the waves, and it was completely calm.*
>
> *The men were amazed and asked, "What kind of man is this? Even the winds and the waves obey him!" (Matthew 8:23–27)*

Jesus is the picture of how perfect faith looks. What is Jesus doing as the storm hits and grows in ferocity until the waves go over the boat? He's asleep. At rest. He had great faith, mature faith. Mature faith is at perfect peace in the midst of the storm.

But the disciples show us what little faith looks like. The storm rages to a level that frightens these weathered fishermen, who are familiar with the ways of the wind on the sea. Have you ever heard anyone say that on an airplane they watch the reaction of the flight crew to know whether to worry? These guys would have been the ones you watch when you were out on a boat at sea. And they were panicked. The narrative describes a storm that would naturally elicit fear. Fear would be a reasonable response to the situation. The disciples did not demonstrate any admirable courage or faith. They were no heroes. They proclaimed the truth as they saw it: "We're going to die!"

At their cry, Jesus got up and calmed the storm with a word. What a miracle! The disciples, who spent day and night with Him, were stunned.

What did it take to access this spectacular miracle? Did it take great faith? No, it took "little faith." Jesus called them "you of little faith." But a little faith was all it took. Enough faith to turn toward Jesus was all the faith required to still a raging storm. Their faith would grow. They would become men of great faith. But even when they were men of little faith, their little faith turned them to Jesus, and Jesus knew just what to do.

Is your faith little? Little is big enough. Don't let the enemy intimidate you out of praying by accusing you of not having enough faith.

THE LYING LIAR

The lie that your spiritual enemy wants you to believe is skillfully drawn to obscure this specific truth: God loves your presence. He has designed prayer so that intimacy will be its primary component. If you believe that God is disappointed in you, or angry with you, or dismissive of you, then you will avoid the intimacy prayer offers because it will make you feel like a failure. You will always be trying to get it right and feeling that, instead, you got it wrong. In *Prayer*, Ole Hallesby wrote:

> Prayer is something deeper than words. It is present in the soul before it has been formulated in words. And it abides in the soul after the last words of prayer have passed over our lips.

Every thought or belief that causes you to feel diminished in God's eyes or dismissed in His presence, is a lie. It feels like the truth, but it is a lie. A lie can only be overcome with truth.

REFRAME

Has your experience of prayer been diminished because you have felt inadequate? Stop and ponder for a minute whether you keep distance from God because you believe that He would not ecstatically welcome a person with your flaws. Admit that you have believed a lie until now.

REFOCUS

Embrace the truth that has been obscured by the lie you have believed. Write out your statement of the truth and every time the lie exerts itself, overlay it with the truth until the lie no longer surfaces.

CHALLENGE FOUR

Trying to follow someone else's pattern for prayer and feeling that you fall short

THE HOLY SPIRIT IS IN ON THE CONVERSATION

God has created you with a unique personality type and your own ways of expressing yourself. The forms of prayer or the structures for a devotional time that work for another person may not fit you at all. God delights in you and in your expressions of prayer.

You are God's workmanship, His art project. He formed every detail according to a plan laid out from the beginning. Nothing about you is accidental or random. He made you as you are. You don't have to fit into anyone else's mold. You can learn from others whom you admire. You can let God refine you and fine-tune you. But you don't need to become someone else.

Just as you relate and interact to others according to your own unique personality and outlook, so your expression of prayer will not be like someone else's. There is no standard for how prayer must be formulated or put into words. There is no one-size-fits-all rule for how a daily time of prayer has to flow. You may have heard lessons or messages about how to organize a complicated prayer life, or you may have bought notebooks and journals to follow a system someone has devised that works for them. Nothing wrong with any of that. However, it might not have fit your personality. So your resolve didn't hold, and you now feel like a failure every time you come across one of these tools at the bottom of a pile.

Let me clarify that I am not criticizing these plans and systems. For some, they work beautifully, and some people stay on track with them for a lifetime. If your personality fits well into structures, you should not try to be like your more freewheeling friend who might describe and experience prayer in an entirely different way. Be who you are, and don't measure yourself against others.

PRAYING FROM YOUR PERSONALITY

I don't do well with schedules and plans and structures in any area of my life. For years, I tried to make myself fit that mold and felt guilty much of the time. It was not wasted time. I learned a lot about what I'm not and that I could never be anyone other than myself. In contrast to the years of trying to pray in someone else's mold, I realize the freedom of praying as me.

Are you a loosey-goosey kind of person trying to be a rules-and-regulations kind of person? Has it worn you out and made prayer a burden? Or are you a person whose productive mode is structured and organized? Have you worried that you are not spontaneous enough? Have you felt that you are less spiritual than another person who approaches prayer in a more unstructured way? Let it go. Pray as you.

For many, our earliest experiences with prayer were listening to others pray. Maybe in church settings you listened to long, droning, flowery prayers peppered with "thees and thous" and standardized prayer terminology. These prayers seemed more like performances and did not draw your heart into prayer. I am not dismissing those prayers because they were likely sincere prayers, and God did not grade them. But they did not model a wide variety of ways to express prayer.

My mother, though, held prayer groups at our house, and I overheard prayers that sounded like conversation. People were not using their prayer voices or using words they didn't use in real life. Prayer flowed as naturally as an informal discussion.

Let's look at how prayer can be as natural as conversing with our dearest friend. No special wordiness is required. You don't have to measure your words or evaluate your ideas before laying them out. Just easy, natural give-and-take, ebb-and-flow. Prayer is expressed in private times of prayer and in groups where people are gathered to pray together or in settings where a formal prayer may be part of the proceedings. In any of these settings, pray as you.

PRIVATE PRAYER

Your times of private prayer do not have to fit anyone else's format. We're going to discuss this in more detail in the next chapter, so I'll just touch on it here.

As an example, I am a person with the kind of temperament that can spend long spans of time being still and quiet. I have a whole world of thoughts and can live inside my own head. I just returned from a week alone in an isolated, remote cabin, and that is my favorite kind of getaway. I'm a hermit by nature. This personality and temperament of mine defines my times of private prayer. I don't have lists. I have a journal I use on occasion, but I have no rules about what goes in it or how often I write in it. I use Scripture, but I don't always read it out of a printed, bound Bible. I don't always read it. Sometimes I listen to it. Sometimes I recall it. I let Scripture spark my praying.

Some days are much more praising and rejoicing, and some are about asking and bringing needs. And some are agonizing over difficulties and getting the Lord's perspective and hearing His promises.

I pray in pictures often. How do I pray in pictures? I realized long ago that God deliberately created us to be visual thinkers and that our brains are capable of seeing images that are not in front of our eyes. He describes in lush detail how His presence looks in books like Revelation, Daniel, and Ezekiel. We don't have to make anything up. I know that prayer moves me into His very presence and affords me His full attentions. Sometimes I just let my heart see that setting. Or, when I think about my children and grandchildren and daughters-in-law, I let my heart see them with the presence of Jesus with them. That is reality. I'm not trying to make it up. I just say their names and glance at the picture in my brain. I just employ God's design for my brain to think in pictures, and I pray in pictures.

That's a taste of how my private times of prayer might go because that is how I'm wired. Now let's talk about how your private prayertimes might go if you are of a different bent. My friend Mary Rose is the opposite of me. She loves everything labeled and filed and calendared and listed. Her freedom is in structure.

What does her private prayertime look like? She has a prayer list (not a to-do list for God) that is dated and written in nice, neat handwriting. She has years' worth of these lists, and they are amazing. She can look back over God's activity in her life on paper. She has a Bible reading plan that she follows, and her structured, planned-out times in His Word yields a living encounter with Him. She uses devotional books. She writes things down throughout the day and brings them into her focused daily prayertime.

Another friend is an off-the-charts extrovert. She is all about people and relationships. Her times of private prayer often end up being times of calling or texting or writing notes because people come to mind. I can't list the many times she has called or texted me during her times of prayer and the message was so precisely what I needed to hear just then.

You get the picture. Your private times of prayer will look like your personality. Feel free to pray as you. If your times of private prayer feel more like an obligation than a delight, very possibly you are trying to emulate someone else's style.

GROUP PRAYER

I have much to say about the value of being part of a small prayer group or a prayer partnership. I'll just touch on it here. This setting is where often that fear of not fitting the right prayer mold comes into play and robs people of this powerful experience.

First, the Scripture tells us that there is a dimension of power in prayer that is accessed by gathered believers seeking God together. "Again, truly I tell you that if two of you on earth agree about anything they ask for, it will be done for them by my Father in heaven. For where two or three gather in my name, there am I with them" (Matthew 18:19–20).

Second, there is a bond that happens among people whose hearts are all attuned to God, in agreement with what God desires. You develop a commitment to one another that is different than what might occur in any other kind of grouping. It is precious and valuable.

I want to encourage you not to let anything hold you back from joining with others in concerted prayer. It does not come naturally. You will feel vulnerable and exposed at first. It will take some time and practice to feel like a group instead of a collection of individuals. But stick with it because in this setting you will learn things about the power of prayer that you will not learn anywhere else. This is the setting in which you will learn how the Holy Spirit works among His people in a unique way, binding our hearts together like nothing else. You will come to deeply love people you pray with when your per-sonalities might not have found common ground anywhere else. You may find that people you may have been angry at or have been hurt by will become people you love and fully trust.

Paul talks about "the riches of his glorious inheritance in his holy people" (Ephesians 5:18). God's riches are on deposit in His people. When we put ourselves in position to be in deep relationships with His people, we mine those riches. Lives flow together like tributaries converging in a river.

In small prayer groups, the different prayer styles of different personality types is one of the great assets. I urge you not to rob your group of your true self in prayer. Remember, you are having a conversation. You are all participants, along with the Holy Spirit. In conversation, you typically don't jump from subject to subject, but you stay on one subject until everyone has expressed himself on it. So it is in a prayer group. Put a need or a topic out and everyone prays through it (like you would talk through it) until everyone feels finished. The Spirit is giving direction, awakening thoughts, prompting ideas. He is at the heart of the conversation.

In conversations, some people are more talkative than others. Some people tend to stay quiet and listen and others speak out. It will be the same in prayer group. Just like in a conversation, you can enter in as many times as you like. You can say just one short prayer and add to it later as something comes to mind. You are not inserting opinion, but rather you are being prompted by the Holy Spirit. Some people might get emotional or tearful as they pray, just like in life some people tend to tear up when they talk. It is not a measure of intensity.

A prayer group is not about going around in a circle and taking turns. You don't need to feel put on the spot. Don't judge yourself or any other member of the group. Let each person be himself or herself. With time, the flow becomes more natural for you. You might begin by sharing with one another about a need or something going on in your life, and it naturally turns into prayer. No one has to announce, "Let's pray about this." Your whole conversation, even when directed to one another, has been prayer. The Holy Spirit is in on the conversation.

If someone else prays what you had in mind to pray, instead of thinking, *Oh no! She said what I was going to say!* rejoice that the Spirit has brought you into agreement. Like you would in a conversation, you can say something like, "I agree with that," and then go on to say it in your words. Learn to pray conversationally instead of each person praying a whole prayer list at a time. Again, God responds to this style of praying just as powerfully as any style of praying, but for the group you will find it more conducive to learning how to pray together and join hearts if times of small group prayer are more conversational.

In a small prayer group or a prayer partnership, you don't have to mimic anyone else. You don't have to say the right things. You are free to pray as you.

Remember that you can move back and forth from addressing prayer to God and having conversation among yourselves. I usually start by spending a few moments focusing on the fact that Jesus is right here and present with us, and by inviting the Holy Spirit to direct our thoughts. Give time for the group to pray as led around that topic.

Then ask for one person who wants to share a need or burden. As you grow into a group, you may have to remind members that prayer requests don't have to be something dramatic. I usually say something like, "How can we support you in prayer this week?" One challenge is to move prayer requests beyond prayers for health needs. Sometimes that is the only kind of prayer request people new to small group praying feel comfortable making, but make an effort to grow past that.

Don't take a list of requests all at once. Instead, take one request and pray conversationally about that until it seems that everyone is finished. I sometimes will even ask, "Does everyone feel finished?" Then have someone designated to close that prayer in a simple sentence like, "Father, this we commit to You." Then take another request and do the same.

Sometimes when someone has a request, I will ask, "Is anyone else dealing with a similar struggle?" and do a category of need. It is meaningful to ask the person or persons for whose request you are about to pray to sit in a chair in the middle of the group and let the group gather around them.

You might also have a pattern of opening prayer on any request with a time first of praise and thanksgiving and then move into praying for that need as the Holy Spirit directs. Many times Scripture will come to mind, and someone will quote or even look up and read Scripture. Someone else might lead out in singing a chorus that comes to mind.

If no one has a particular prayer request, the leader could introduce topics: children, spouses, neighbors, world events, pastors, schoolteachers. This is sometimes a good way to get off the ground and let that comfort level with each other grow.

Another great advantage to small prayer groups is that this is the place where you can bring that ongoing request that you feel like others might be tired of hearing. Your group will stand with you in prayer as long as it takes. In your small prayer group, you can bring the same request to every meeting and your group will help bear your burden.

PUBLIC PRAYER

Some occasions call for one person to lead a public prayer. In this instance, it depends on the setting how that prayer might be expressed, but still you are not putting on a performance. And there is not a particular way a prayer has to be articulated.

In an occasion of public prayer, the person voicing prayer is leading the congregation or audience in prayer. Directing thoughts Godward, not just speaking his or her own personal agenda.

A public prayer might be impromptu. The person may be seasoned at praying in public and so perfectly comfortable letting the Holy Spirit lead his thoughts. In those kinds of situations, if you heard me praying aloud in an impromptu setting, you would hear me pause sometimes and grapple for the words sometimes because I am trying to be present to the Spirit in that moment. It doesn't make me feel uncomfortable to be less than smooth in my praying. I could certainly pull phrases out of a hat if I wanted, and sound much more polished, but I don't care about that. But then, that's me. I'm loosey-goosey, remember? Someone else might feel so distracted by being that off-the-cuff and would have a more genuine expression of prayer by having some topics and words ready. That doesn't make that person less attentive to the Spirit. The Spirit is perfectly capable of disclosing in advance what His heart wants to express. Pray as you.

In more formal and structured settings, it is a good idea to have your prayer thought out in advance. Again, the fact that you asked the Spirit beforehand to guide your thoughts and share His heart through you doesn't undermine the power in the moment. If you see a person praying publicly from notes, don't automatically assume they are playing to the audience. God doesn't grade us on prayer, so let's not grade each other. Pray as you.

JUST AS YOU ARE

In your prayerful relationship to God, you can find the most authentic you. You have nothing to hide and no one to impress. You can relax in knowing that you are adored just as you are.

That your presence is a joy to the Father. That when it comes to prayer, you can't get it wrong.

As His carefully designed creation, you give Him joy. When He sees you, He sees His own beautiful project. He designed all your quirks and the bent of your personality. I think He sometimes turns to the angels and says something like, "Hey! Look what I made!"

REFRAME

In what settings have you felt anxious about how to pray or inadequate about your praying? Is it possible that your enemy is strategically discouraging you from the very settings where you will see prayer's power in new ways? What step can you take to deliberately overcome your prayer anxiety?

REFOCUS

Deliberately set your mind on truth: that God delights in how He has created you and loves when you pray as you. Every time a fear-based lie surfaces in your thoughts, stop and mentally sit still and feel the Father's joy in you. Bask for a moment in His love and acceptance.

CHALLENGE FIVE

Feeling that in one time frame—maybe you call it a quiet time—you have to fit in everything included in a predetermined prayer formula

LET LOVE RUN THE SHOW

Though prayer is always flowing between your heart and God's, we do still need to commit daily times for focused prayer. No way around it, this grounds the relationship and requires commitment that does not come naturally. A praying life does not exclude daily disciplined times of prayer. These are the times that undergird and nourish a praying life.

However, let's make sure we understand what these times are for. This is not your one shot at God. This is not the time to get all your orders in to the heavenly warehouse before He runs out of exactly what you want.

This time is a love commitment. It is a time when He is your undistracted focus. You are opening your life and your heart to Him, allowing Him access to you so that He can accomplish what only He can do. Every time you choose time with Him over the many things that could be filling that space, you are acting on your words of love to Him. Every obedient action is an expression of love to Him, backing up your words with your actions. Don't be like those God describes as drawing near with their mouths but keeping hearts far away.

"These people come near to me with their mouth
and honor me with their lips, but their hearts
are far from me. Their worship of me is based

on merely human rules they have been taught"
(Isaiah 29:13).

Consider that daily time of prayer the most important thing you will do all day. It is a love gift to the Father, and it is a gift you give to those you love and whose lives have been entrusted to you. Here, you will move toward being the best version of yourself. Here, you will bring them and the details of their lives into heaven's throne room.

This is where you may find outlines helpful, even if you are an unstructured style pray-er. You don't have to pray according to an outline or a formula, but prayer outlines can be helpful if you keep them in the right perspective. Let them function to keep you focused when necessary but not to become a legalistic burden. When you remember that you are living in a prayerful relationship, you will recognize that in the course of your praying life you are incorporating all the aspects of prayer; likewise, you will be freed of needing to "cover all the bases" every time you set aside time for focused prayer. If you use a prayer outline, learn to use it as a starting point but not an end in itself.

To avoid feeling like you won't know how to fill the time you have dedicated to focusing on the Lord, let a prayer outline be a resource. Let me suggest Jesus' very practical teaching on daily disciplined prayer.

"But when you pray, go into your room, close the door and pray to your Father, who is unseen. Then your Father, who sees what is done in secret, will reward you" (Matthew 6:6).

THE HABIT

"When you pray . . ." We must have the habit of praying. A habit is an action that has become fixed in your life through repetition. The decision to perform a habit is settled. You don't have to refight the battle. Develop the habit of daily prayer, preferably as the first action of your day.

> *"In the morning, L*ORD*, you hear my voice; in the morning I lay my requests before you and wait expectantly" (Psalm 5:3).*

> *"Let the morning bring me word of your unfailing love, for I have put my trust in you. Show me the way I should go, for to you I entrust my life" (Psalm 143:8).*

> *"He wakens me morning by morning, wakens my ear to listen like one being instructed" (Isaiah 50:4).*

Early morning, before the demands and distractions of the day, is prime time for being focused in the Lord's presence. It sets the tone for the day. It establishes your priority for the day. There are scheduling issues and seasons of life that make early morning impossible, and that does not devalue your prayertime. But, if the choice of early morning is available, make that choice.

Decide how much time you will commit to that daily prayertime, and stick to that commitment. Will you commit an hour? Thirty minutes? Fifteen minutes? Whatever you decide, keep that commitment.

THE PLACE

"When you pray . . . go into your room and close the door." As part of establishing the habit of daily prayer, we should, as often as possible, use the same location. By choosing a designated location, you will have one less decision to make. You can have your Bible and prayer journal, or whatever materials you use, already in place. The more routine the outward behaviors are, the more energy is focused on the inward activities. When you don't have to give thought to the functional details, you will come to prayer less distracted, more ready to listen to Him. When you enter into your room, you are to shut the door. You need to choose a place where life's distractions will be less likely to infringe. Your location should not become so important, though, that you feel you can miss your prayertime if your location is not available. The true location of your prayer is within you. If the same space each day is unrealistic for you— have a quiet time bag. Have everything in your bag that you use during your prayertime, and have the bag with you so you can set up sacred space on the go.

THE FOCUS

"When you pray . . . pray to your Father, who is unseen." The purpose of your prayertime is to give God your undivided attention. It is not for the purpose of securing His favor for the day. His favor rests on you forever. A daily prayertime should not be viewed superstitiously. Sometimes I hear people say something like, "When I have a prayertime, my day goes well. When I skip it, I have a bad day." Daily prayer is not a magic powder to sprinkle on your day. If you have a habit of daily prayer, it will be followed by some good days and some bad days. The difference will be that you will be centered in God and will react differently to both good and bad. The focus of your prayertime is God Himself. This is not your one chance to get His attention. You will be walking in prayer all day and all night. You don't have to feel compelled to get all your prayer requests in at this time, as if this will be your only chance. The agenda for your daily prayertime is to hear God, to reaffirm His rule in your life.

THE RESPONSE

"When you pray . . . Your Father, who sees what is done in secret, will reward you." Jesus said that those who pray so that others will admire them will have the reward they seek. Their spiritual lives may well be applauded and admired. However, they will have settled for a cheap reward. They will not be rewarded with the presence of God. Theirs will be a perishable crown. The reward God offers is Himself, and that will be more than enough. In His presence we find everything we are looking for. He is our very great reward.

NO ROLE PLAYING

I like how Eugene Peterson translates this passage, Matthew 6:6–9, in *The Message.*

> Here's what I want you to do: Find a quiet, secluded place so you won't be tempted to role-play before God. Just be there as simply and honestly as you can manage. The focus will shift from you to God, and you will begin to sense his grace.
>
> The world is full of so-called prayer warriors who are prayer-ignorant. They're full of formulas and programs and advice, peddling techniques for getting what you want from God. Don't fall for that nonsense. This is your Father you are dealing with, and He knows better than you what you need. With a God like this loving you, you can pray very simply.

These are the words with which Jesus introduces the Lord's Prayer or the Model Prayer. He warns us away from formulas meant to get God to do what we tell Him to do. Yet, He gives us an outline of sorts. He suggests some structure for our guidance while warning us away from thinking of payer as a formula to get right.

In His Model Prayer, He gives bullet points for what prayer as a whole covers. He doesn't say to be sure you get all these topics in every single time you set aside time specifically for prayer. In the course of your praying life, all these topics will have expression.

There is something to be gleaned from each bullet point and the order in which He places them. Again, a prayer outline is helpful as a tool as long as it functions as a tool and not as the machine that runs the show.

LIKE THIS

"Our Father in heaven, hallowed be your name,"

Making the fatherhood of God your opening thought brings you right where the Father wants you. Aware of His tender, protective, providing love for you. Starting with praise gets your mind focused on His power and greatness before you begin to look at your needs. Perspective is everything.

"Your kingdom come, your will be done
on earth as it is in heaven."

Next, Jesus invites us to intercession—to use the power of prayer as the conduit through which the supply and the provision of heaven flows into the circumstances of earth. For each need or concern, simply pray heaven's power into earth's events.

"Give us today our daily bread."

Simply ask God to provide for your daily needs. Be as specific in naming those needs as you can. As you name your daily needs, release them to Him. Trust Him.

"Forgive us our debts, as we also have forgiven our debtors."

Give God time to bring to your attention anyone whom you have hurt so that you can make amends. Ask Him to show you anyone against whom you are holding anger, and ask Him to free you of the bitterness or resentment that has you bound.

"And lead us not into temptation, but deliver us from the evil one."

Jesus' prayer outline teaches us to ask for deliverance from the evil one—rescue us from the lies and distortions of the evil one. Let the Holy Spirit show you any area of your life in which you are aligning your life with the enemy's lies instead of the Father's truth.

INTEGRATE SCRIPTURE

Let the Word of God define your times of prayer. Scripture is where His thoughts toward you are revealed, and He speaks His love for you directly from the pages of Scripture to your heart. Scripture is where He speaks His living, active word into your life and awakens desires and longings that He has authored in you.

I have developed seven methods I use when reading Scripture devotionally that help me hear the Living Voice in the Word. Use the ones that resonate with you. Here is a brief summary of how I listen for God in His Word.

1. Read a portion of Scripture. Go slowly. Any time a thought captures your attention, stop and reread it. Underline it. Give it time to soak in. Read the thought several times, each time putting the emphasis on a different word.

2. Take the Scripture passage apart, and look at each piece separately. Write down each phrase. Beside it, write down your own sense of what that phrase is saying to you. Pay particular attention to phrases and words such as *if . . . then, so that, because, therefore, but, and,* and *when.* Underline or circle these words, and consider how they reveal connections or cause-and-effect relationships.

3. Let me introduce you to what I call my *Jeopardy* method. *Jeopardy* is a popular game in which the player, having been given the answer, must supply the question. Look at the Scripture and ask yourself: "What questions does this passage answer?" List the questions and the answers. I usually go phrase by phrase or thought by thought. When you are finished, look back through your list. You will see new angles to the truth.

4. As you experience the Scripture, what has God said directly to you? Write down your name, then write what you are hearing God say. For example, I might write down, "Darling Jennifer," or "Beloved Daughter," or "Apple of My Eye," or any endearment I hear Him use toward me. Then I write out His personal Word to me from Scripture. Take time to enjoy His passionate, tender love for you. Even when His Word to you is a Word of correction or reproof, it is loving and gentle.

5. Write your honest, heartfelt response to God. In your private time with Him, learn to use terms of endearment. Call Him "Daddy," like Jesus did. Call Him "My Greatest Love," "Beloved," or "My Life." Learn to be lovingly intimate and at ease with Him. Sometimes your response may be loving and faith-filled. Sometimes it may be confusion, or doubt, or even anger and frustration. Be honest. God is not fragile.

His love for you is absolutely steadfast, immovable, never wavering. You can trust Him to love you unconditionally.

6. Based on your experience with Scripture, what assurances or promises has God made you in His Word? Write them down. Pray these promises as the Holy Spirit applies them to people or situations He has assigned to you for intercession. Write the name or situation next to the promise. Date it. Think of this exercise as harvesting each promise and praying it into that life or situation. When the Father says in His Word that all of His promises are already yes in Christ, that causes me to picture a field of ripe and ready grain. The grain is ready to harvest. When we pray based on God's promises, we are harvesting those promises. You do not have to watch to see if God will fulfill His Word. Instead, watch to see how God is fulfilling His Word.

7. As you read stories and events from Scripture, put yourself there in real time in your imagination. Imagine how the story would unfold to you if you were experiencing it in real time instead of reading an account. Get a fresh view of Jesus.

PRAYERTIME AS LISTENING TIME

The primary reason for set aside times of prayer is to listen to God. We hear God most reliably in His Word. He has set things up so that the deep transforming truths in the Scripture are not sitting on the surface to be skimmed off by the casual observer. Instead, the wonderful, rich, consecrating truth is buried and must be mined, like gold or silver.

> *If you call out for insight and cry aloud for under-standing, and if you look for it as for silver and search for it as for hidden treasure, then you will understand the fear of the LORD and find the knowledge of God. For the LORD gives wisdom, and from his mouth come knowledge and under-standing. (Proverbs 2:3–6)*

Why is the deep truth hidden? Why can't the treasures of wisdom and knowledge be readily accessible to any person's intellect?

God has deliberately hidden deep truth so that the Holy Spirit, the Spirit of truth, can disclose it. "For whatever is hidden is meant to be disclosed, and whatever is concealed is meant to be brought out into the open" (Mark 4:22). The truths of God's Word are buried for one purpose—so that you and I can find them.

In the process of revealing "deep and hidden things" (Daniel 2:22), God anchors in His children the knowledge that we are totally dependent upon Him. Even our understanding of the truth comes directly and only from Him. Left to our own devices, we will never see any deeper than the surface. In the course of learning directly from Him, intimacy is strengthened and enriched. Our hunger, our longing, is really for Him.

> We might have expected, we may think we should have preferred, an unrefracted light giving us ulti-mate truth in systematic form—something we could have tabulated and memorised and relied on like a multiplication table. . . . God must have done what is best, this is best, therefore God has done this.
>
> It may be indispensable that Our Lord's teach-ing, by its elusiveness (to our systematising intel-lect), should demand a response from the whole man, should make it so clear that there is no ques-tion of learning a subject but of steeping ourselves in a Personality. (C. S. Lewis, *Reflections on the Psalms*)

As you engage with God during your time of private prayer, steep yourself in Him through His Word, as C. S. Lewis says. Marinate. Soak.

Meditate on Scripture continually, letting it flood you and fill you until it forms an outgoing current called prayer. Meditating on a passage and mining its hidden riches will be only the beginning. You will not discover all the riches stored there in a sitting. You will be depositing His Word in your mind so that He can continually make withdrawals from it. As you marinate your life in His truth, the Spirit will make connections between passages. You will notice a thread of truth running through the Word. Suddenly, at an unexpected moment, God will shine a search light on a truth from a Scripture you thought you had already mined. You will see something clearly that you had not noticed or put together before. It will be so plain that you will wonder how it escaped you. The key is to keep depositing the Word.

SLOW DOWN YOUR PRAYERTIME

Don't let your times of prayer be hijacked by the feeling of frenzied attempts to get it right or to fit everything in. Let these times be a fret-free zone. Sometimes you won't feel like having that time, but don't let feelings run the show. Let love run the show.

During your quiet time of prayer, you are open to the voice of God in a particular way that is unique to this set aside time. God can unlock the secrets of the kingdom for you as He has your full attention. We've already seen that the riches He has stored in the secret places can only be revealed to your understanding by the direct action of His Spirit on your mind. The truth is encrypted in God's Word.

Encrypted is a computer technology word that means "to convert plain text into unintelligible form by means of a code." Once text has been encrypted, any person who does not have the correct password will only see unintelligible text. Only those specially designated individuals who have been given the password can read encrypted information. The password is the key that unlocks the secrets in the document. Enter the password, and the unintelligible text becomes plain text. The truth in God's Word is encrypted, and only the children of the kingdom have the key.

"The secret of the kingdom of God has been given to you. But to those on the outside everything is said in parables so that, 'they may be ever seeing, but never perceiving, and ever hearing but never understanding'" (Mark 4:11–12).

Do you see? You have been given the key that unlocks the kingdom's secrets. The Spirit, working directly in your mind and understanding, reveals truth. First Corinthians 2:12 tells you that God has given you His Spirit for this purpose: "that [you] might understand what God has freely given [you]." Because you have the Holy Spirit, you can understand what the human intellect alone is unable to comprehend.

The full, substantive, mature truth is hidden from the world to be revealed to those in whom the Spirit dwells. The Spirit-led life is the continual and progressive apprehension of deeper and deeper levels of truth. "Call to me and I will answer you and tell you great and unsearchable things you do not know" (Jeremiah 33:3). He will tell you truths that are beyond the ordinary (great) and inaccessible (unsearchable). The secrets of the kingdom are His to reveal.

In your times of focused prayer, be more concerned about being alert to the presence of God and what He wants to impart to you than you are concerned about fitting everything into your time frame. You can't go wrong when you come to Him for the purpose of knowing more truth, and of walking closer to His heart.

To recap, you don't have to cram everything into every scheduled time of prayer. Use an outline of prayer to keep you focused or to get you started, but don't become enslaved to it. Sit back and relax, and let the Holy Spirit give definition and structure to your time of prayer. Over the course of your praying life, as you interact with Jesus through every minute of your day, incorporate all the bullet points Jesus taught. Make sure that you remember to praise and worship Him. Revel in the fact that He is your Father. Ask for the things you need. Bring everything to Him, asking for heaven to intervene on earth. Be vulnerable to His conviction of sin so He can free you of sin's warping influence. Be tender toward those who have hurt and offended you, and respond when the Spirit brings those very ones to mind. Leave your enemy defeated and in the dust by allowing God to keep unmasking his lies and pointing you to the truth. This is a teaching for your lifetime, not just your quiet time.

REFRAME

Consider what the purpose of a daily set-aside time of prayer is. How would you state it? How does this free you from feeling pressured to get through an outline for prayer in order for it to count?

REFOCUS

Be purposeful about incorporating all of Jesus' points in the Model Prayer into the totality of your praying life. Which do you skimp on? How will you start building up the weak places?

CHALLENGE SIX

Being stuck in a prayer rut

REPLACE THEM WITH RITUALS THAT HAVE MEANING

Do you feel like you are stuck in a rut? Has prayer become a duty rather than a delight? Are you lacking the joy you once had in prayer? Do you feel like you are just going through the motions?

Let me say that even if you answer yes to these questions, the fact that you are still praying matters. The measure of prayer is not how you feel when you engage in it. But God does want you to find delight in His presence and in the prayer relationship. Let's look at some practical ways you can infuse your experience of prayer with new life.

REPETITION

One of the things that might make you feel like you're in a rut is when you say the same prayer in the same words over and over.

There is nothing wrong with this. These may be words that the Spirit has etched in your heart, and each time the person or situation comes to mind, or when you pray deliberately about it during specific prayertimes, those very words or phrases surface in your mind. They are powerful, Spirit-inspired words that, when spoken in prayer, move the situation forward. Prayer requires perseverance, so persevere. Don't devalue the way you are wording prayer simply because you are saying it in the same words. That does not disqualify it as powerful prayer. Instead, embrace those words and let the power and promise in them flow afresh in your heart each time you lift them in prayer. Perseverance in prayer is a key component. Jesus taught much about the need for perseverance. For example, in Luke 18:1, Luke explains that the point of Jesus' parable was to persevere: "Then Jesus told his disciples a parable to show them that they should always pray and not give up." He instructs in Matthew 7:7 (AMP), "Keep on asking and it will be given you; keep on seeking and you will find; keep on knocking [reverently] and [the door] will be opened to you." Prayer is having effect even when you can't see that effect. If perseverance is expressed in the same words or phrases, it doesn't matter.

If you come to a person and make a request in the same words day after day, we call that nagging. Perseverance is not nagging. When you make that same request of a person, you are likely trying to wear him down, or persuade him, or make sure he doesn't forget. But in prayer you are doing none of those things. You are cooperating with God in moving His power and provision into the circumstances of earth. You are reaching into the heavenly realms and grabbing hold of God's power and pulling it onto the earth.

So, pray on. God is authoring your prayer. Don't see prayer as words you made up and are directing at God, but rather see them as words God has planted in you.

On the other hand, there is nothing wrong with varying the way you express the same longing or desire in prayer. As a writer, I am always on a mission to pin down exactly the right word. There are times when a different word that means the same thing just brings some new spark or insight. Ask the Lord if He would supply a word that would freshen up your prayer. (This would be for your sake, not His. He isn't waiting for you to hit on the right word.) Use an online (or print) thesaurus or dictionary to look up your word and see what alternatives come up. Or, wait on the Lord to suggest another word or phrase to your mind, likely through your ongoing intake of His Word. It will just jump off the page one day. Alternatively, if you are using words that come from the pages of Scripture, look up that Scripture in other translations and see if you get a new view of what you are praying.

If your repetition comes out of a stubborn insistence that God must do things a certain way in order to meet your expectations, then that is what I believe Jesus meant by "vain repetitions" (Matthew 6:7 NKJV) or "meaningless repetition" (NASB). Look at the context of this phrase: "And when you pray, do not heap up empty phrases as the Gentiles do, for they think that they will be heard for their many words" (Matthew 6:7 ESV). In meaningless repetition, the petitioner believes his "many words" will win him some favor from God. The problem is not that he uses many words, but that he thinks his words will give his prayer clout. He believes that he can win God over to his point of view with much talking. So, his words are empty. They are not Spirit-inspired words, so they have no heft to them. He sounds consequential, with his prodigious, long-winded verbosity. But Jesus says he's a lightweight in the spiritual realm. You—with a few awkward words—have more pull in heaven than the one who heaps up empty phrases.

Meaningless repetition is different from persevering prayer, and only you and the Lord know which is which. You will not find a formula against which to measure. However, I would make a few suggestions for you to consider.

1. First, be willing for the Lord to reveal to you His answer to this question: "Lord, is this meaningless repletion or faith-fueled perseverance? Show me my own heart." Then trust Him to do so. Don't agonize or struggle, just be open. Often, to such questions, His answer is not immediate but instead unfolds over some time.

2. If the content of your prayer is a laundry list of ways that God must perform and a time frame in which He must perform, then are you willing to lay every expectation and demand down? Are you willing to fully surrender to His plan, even if it does not align with yours? Do you trust that His plan is for your benefit and is birthed out of His love for you and any other of your loved ones impacted in your situation?

3. Does your experience with this repeated prayer leave you frustrated or fearful rather than released? When this is my experience over time, I have come to realize that I am

trying hard to get God in line. I have to stop and surrender every idea, every longing, every need to Him to work out in His way in His time. When the peace of God fills me, I know I have given up my empty insistence on my own way.

Try this experiment. Write down the prayer in which you are persevering. Every detail as you want to see it worked out. Then—maybe with red marker for emphasis— overlay your expectations and desires with the word *surrendered*. Date it. I like tangible actions in a moment of struggle. It just helps me experience the reality. And I have a record of what I surrendered and when. I have many of these moments in my years of prayer journals. When I look back at what I thought had to happen for life to be happy, overlaid with my surrender, the record reveals that God is better at knowing than I am. Always.

BOREDOM

Sometimes when we do everything the same way all the time for stretches of time, a certain boredom sets in. This doesn't mean you are bored with God—or with prayer. Sameness sometimes brings a sense of being on autopilot, not fully invested in the moment. I'm all for having a set time and place to cut down on complications that might distract us from the discipline, but that doesn't exclude varying our rituals.

If you are struggling with boredom, consider some of these ideas. Vary your forms of praying. Find ways to liven up your prayer experiences. Ask the Lord to give you ideas. For an extensive list of ideas, see my book *Live a Praying Life in Adversity*, where I list 52 different ways to pray, each to be practiced for a week at a time.

1. Sing your prayers sometimes. No one is listening but God. Your prayer songs don't have to have either rhyme or rhythm. If this sounds silly to you right now, just try it. You'll see that it just engages you differently.

2. Sing hymns or praise choruses, or even listen to recorded praise music and enter in with all your heart. As you are joining your heart with the words of the songs, specific people and situations you are praying about will come to mind, and the words will help you express your heart.

3. Walk through your house and pray room by room sometimes.

4. Prayerwalk your neighborhood, letting the familiar sights trigger prayer.

5. Just do physical activity such as walking, jogging, treadmilling, or the like as you pray. Years ago, my mother used to walk a track for exercise, and that was her focused prayertime. Basically, she would pray for one person on her heart for one lap, then change topics at the next lap.

She found that it kept her focused. All of us whose lives were the content of her prayers knew exactly what she meant when she said, "I gave you an extra lap today."

6. Write a note, an email, or a text of a prayer for a person on your heart. Do more than say, "I prayed for you." Consider writing out your prayer. With today's technology, you could even record a prayer in an audio file and text or email it.

The Lord is endlessly creative and knows you and your personality. Just ask Him. Don't feel guilty about feeling bored, and then feel free to express yourself without restraint.

SELF-ABSORPTION

Prayer is about God. It is a response to His wooing, and it is the force that accomplishes His plans. If we make ourselves the center of prayer, it will wear us out. We were not created to be the center or our universe. You were designed to worship God, the true center of the universe. When our focus is on ourselves and the content of our prayers is all about us, we tire under the burden. I wrote about this in *Altar'd*:

> We were built to be God-focused. That's the condi-
> tion under which we thrive. "Since, then, you have
> been raised with Christ, set your hearts on things

above, where Christ is seated at the right hand of God. Set your minds on things above, not on earthly things. For you died, and your life is now hidden with Christ in God" (Colossians 3:1–4). Self-consciousness is not our natural state. No one except God is worthy of such concentrated attention. The proper focus of all aspects of our personality is to put God first (Matthew 6: 33). . . . We were not fashioned to be self-focused. It doesn't work. We break down under it. Why? Because we are not worthy of worship. The world was not created to revolve around you. You can't handle it; it's not your role. We were made to be worshippers.

The reason for your prayer rut might be that you have made prayer all about you. Simple fix. When you begin to make prayer all about God, you will find a new vitality. Here are some suggestions:

1. Use Scripture to get your heart God-focused. Marinate in the Word and let His living, active Word speak life into you. As His Spirit hand-delivers the words of Scripture to your heart, He is speaking the same powerful Word through which He created the earth.

   Consider the words Kathy Howard penned in *Fed Up with Flat Faith*:

Scripture intake should always prompt prayer. As we read and meditate, we should continually respond to what God says to us. For instance, as we read Psalm 51:3—"For I know my transgressions"—the Holy Spirit may point out a specific sin we need to confess. Right then is the time for us to acknowledge our sin to God and repent. Scripture can also be our prayer. No prayer is more eloquent or meaningful than God's own words. Start a list of passages you can use to pray in various life circumstances and for specific needs. For instance, I have a list of Scriptures about spiritual growth I use to pray for myself and others.

Vary the translation of the Bible that you use from time to time. Encountering a familiar passage in new words can spark new thoughts. I have a friend who starts a new translation of the Bible at the beginning of each year. She uses that Bible for one of her several grandchildren each year and she marks it and writes prayers for that grandchild, or promises for his life, or makes notes in the margins. Then she gives that Bible to that grandchild at the end of the year and starts another translation and focuses on another grandchild the next year. Can you imagine the treasure those Bibles are for each of her grandchildren?

Consider using a biblically based devotional book that will point you to Scripture and give encouragement and insight. This doesn't replace your insight in Scripture, but God speaks through His instruments. Another person's perspective will often spark a new thought in you.

2. With each request or situation, start with thanksgiving for everything you can see, and then for those things you can't yet see. Thank Him for what He is doing and for what He will do. Instead of always framing it as a request, pray something like this: "Here is a situation You have allowed to be in my life. Use it for Your intentions and work out good from it as You have always planned." Then let prayer flow from that attitude. As you wrap petition in thanksgiving, the supernatural peace that comes directly from God and is not dependent on the circumstances will stand guard over your heart.

> *"Do not be anxious about anything, but in every situation, by prayer and petition, with thanksgiving, present your requests to God. And the peace of God, which transcends all understanding, will guard your hearts and your minds in Christ Jesus." (Philippians 4:6)*

When Paul says that the peace of God will guard your heart, the word translated "guard" means to stand watch or be on patrol. Peace will be on the lookout for anxiety or worry and route it before it reaches you. This is the amazing power of thanksgiving. So, practice thanksgiving until it is your default mode.

In her book *The Uncluttered Heart: Making Room for God During Advent and Christmas*, Beth A. Richardson wrote, "Living from the perspective of gratitude and joy, our hearts remain open to the Spirit's influence; we stay connected to God's guidance. Being grateful for God's good in our lives displaces our fears and dissatisfactions and replaces them with God's presence."

3. Keep your focus on the Supplier, not the need. Whatever is in the foreground of your thoughts will loom largest. If your difficulty or need takes up the most real estate of your thought life, then it will loom largest. Train your brain to divert thoughts of the need to thoughts of the Supplier. Live a God-focused life of praise.

> *"So we fix our eyes not on what is seen, but on what is unseen, since what is seen is temporary, but what is unseen is eternal" (2 Corinthians 4:18).*

God is the big picture. When He is the focal point, then everything else takes on the proper dimensions. We see things in perspective. Big God. Little circumstances. . . . Refocus. Get God in view. Let yourself be strengthened and enabled. Receive. When we are God focused, we can stand firm. We won't be pushed and shoved by circumstances. We can live lives of courage and integrity. We can let our lives flow in service to others. We don't have to be diminished by events.

—*Life Unhindered! Five Keys to Walking in Freedom*

ROTE RITUAL

We can fall into a nearly superstitious approach to times of focused prayer. We attach meaning to rituals and perform them by rote instead of by heart. Anything can become ritualized. The best and truest things can fall into a meaningless ritual.

There is nothing wrong with a ritual. Rituals can be meaningful. They can give a way to express an invisible spiritual longing in a tangible way. God gave rituals and ceremonies for just that reason. Feasts and celebrations and instructions for worshipping and certain prescribed clothing for priests, for example. But these outward ceremonial rituals were to express inner reality, not to replace real heartfelt worship.

It could be that the remedy for rituals that have become rote is to replace them with rituals that have meaning. Decide to do something that would have a meaning to you. Light a candle. Sing a hymn or chorus. Kneel or bow. Don't do any of this because it might impress God or give you more access to Him. Don't do it because you think it is required. Do it only if you it occurs to you that some outward action would genuinely help you express an inner longing. Sometimes I like to lay my hands physically on a photo of a person for whom I'm praying. I have photos of all my close family members and many of my dear friends. I keep them with my materials I use in my prayertime. This adds no power to prayer, but it helps me enter in fully. I do the same with my calendar sometimes. Or, I often drink my morning coffee during my time of daily prayer, and I have coffee mugs that have connections to people. Sometimes I lift my coffee mug up to the Lord. No one is watching, so I'm free to do things that might look silly to someone else. I lift that mug before the Lord, and He and I know what it means. If a particular verse or passage of Scripture spoke to you, lay your hand on it as you pray it and claim its promise.

When my husband passed away, a dear friend of mine gave me a pair of flannel pajamas with coffee cups all over them because she saw them and, on a whim, they reminded her of my late husband, Wayne. He was always meeting people for coffee or visiting over coffee. Coffee was more than a drink to him. It was a bond. He was a coffee-drinking kind of guy. Nobody had to explain that between us. She gave me the pajamas and said, "These reminded me of Wayne," and no other explanation was needed. In the darkest days of my grief, I would put on the pajamas, and it was a tangible reminder to me that I was swathed in the prayers of my friends. A little ritual that meant nothing to anyone else, but it expressed something to me. Some years later, a dear friend was going through a grief, and I went to my dresser drawer and pulled out my pajamas and said, "Here. I healed in these." They meant an entirely different thing to her than they had to me, but between us, it meant something.

Make up your own rituals. They should fit *you*. They should have meaning for *you*. They are actions or palpable, visible objects that help your either express or experience the reality of the invisible spiritual realm.

REFRAME

Feel free to admit that you feel that your times of prayer have become stuck in a rut. Don't feel guilty. Just determine to take steps to rectify. As you admit your rut, acknowledge that you are not satisfied with that situation and that you desire to fully enjoy your relationship with the Lord. Tell Him so. Write it out.

REFOCUS

Have you identified some reasons why you might feel stuck in a rut? Decide on the actions and readjustments that will get you out of the ditch and back on the road. Determine that you will not be satisfied with less than God has for you. Invest in change so that the relationship will blossom.

CHALLENGE SEVEN

Struggling not to let your mind wander

STAY

This is the most common question I hear: what can I do about my wandering mind?

If your mind wanders, my first suggestion is to feel free to follow it and see where it might be going. Maybe God is trying to lure you out of your tightly controlled agenda and take your prayers in a direction you had not considered.

I am often amused at the track my mind takes that leads from one thought to another. A seemingly random thought meanders here and there and comes out at a concrete idea. Yesterday, for example, I was driving on a country road and smelled a skunk. That reminded me of a high school friend because the first time I ever smelled a skunk was when she and I hit one. The thought of that friend led me to think of another of our mutual high school friends whom I had spoken to recently and who is having a big struggle in her life right now. That caused me to pray for her and to text her that I was thinking of her. (I waited until I pulled off the road, I promise!) She texted back that she was sitting in her doctor's office and had just received difficult news. It all started with smelling a skunk. No matter how random a thought might be, it has the potential to lead you exactly where God wants your mind to go.

"The king's heart is a stream of water in the hand of the LORD; he turns it wherever he will" (Proverbs 21:1 ESV).

As you start your time of focused prayer, let your opening prayer be something like: "Father, I offer You my mind and my thoughts. Direct my thoughts in the direction of Yours. Let my heart and mind be a stream of water in Your hand. Turn it wherever You will."

But there is also an element of disciplining your thoughts to stay in sync with His. Let's look at some of the more common distractions people struggle with and how you might handle these. With your discipline, stay open to the Lord's leading you down unexpected paths.

SPECIFIC DISTRACTIONS

Remember *unfinished tasks or awaiting tasks* is a common distraction.

Keep a list beside you where you can write down these tasks as they come to mind. Listing them assures that you won't forget them. I have a little system I use. I have a form that I designed to go along with my own brain. On my list I have categories like Email, Phone, Bills, and then also project names. I keep it with me all through my workday, not just during my prayertime. As something suddenly occurs to me, I write it down under the category so I don't just end up with a jumbled list of stuff. I know that I will sit down and make phone calls in one sitting, for example. So I have all my phone calls listed in one place. As you list something, release it and ask the Lord's direction and blessing. Even when it is something that seems inconsequential, God is a micromanager—He's in on the details. I even ask such small favors as to get me to the right customer service person when I call about a problem.

Consider the possibility that God is reminding you during your time set aside for prayer because He wants you to lift it to Him. It doesn't have to become a long, drawn-out prayer. Just agree with Him that as you write it down, you are not only making a reminder for yourself but also you are doing an act of releasing it to Him for His purposes. Every step you take, every small action you perform, all are under the Lord's watchful eye.

> "The Lord makes firm the steps of the one who delights in him; though he may stumble, he will not fall, for the Lord upholds him with his hand" (Psalm 37:23–24).

> "You have searched me, Lord, and you know me. You know when I sit and when I rise; you perceive my thoughts from afar. You discern my going out and my lying down; you are familiar with all my ways" (Psalm 139:1–3).

"Does he not see my ways and count my every step?" (Job 31:4).

Sometimes we are distracted by *our own worries and anxieties.* When a worry draws my mind away from deliberate prayer and sucks me into its dark vortex and I suddenly realize that is where I am, I let that direct me back to God. Don't spend any time feeling guilty. Just snap back to the Lord and realize that everything you are worrying about is God's opening to display His power.

Psalm 94:19, translated in New American Standard Version, describes well how anxious thoughts feel. "When my anxious thoughts *multiply* within me, Your consolations delight my soul" (emphasis mine). They multiply. One leads to another, to another, to another. They feed on each other and exacerbate each other. I start with a tiny niggle of concern and find myself in a tsunami of fear. That Hebrew word translated "multiply" here can mean become wealthy, to experience abundance, to become plentiful. Anxious thoughts, left unchecked, get fat and wealthy.

Your enemy wants to take advantage of anxious thoughts to draw your attention away from God and mire you in your own fear. God wants to use those same thoughts to draw you to Himself and comfort you with His promises and His presence. For each anxious thought, God has a promise to counter fear's assault.

I have a phrase that calls me back when I realize my mind

has wandered off into the land of anxiety. I have used it for years. I just pray, "Only You," and immediately my thoughts are back and centered around God and His love for me. It's not a magic phrase. Just some words that express my heart that longs to be with Him. It resets my attitude and puts me in mind of faith instead of fear.

Recall Paul's words from Philippians 4:6. "Do not be anxious about anything, but in every situation, by prayer and petition, with thanksgiving, present your requests to God." The words he uses are extreme, leaving no situation as an exception.

Don't be anxious about *anything*. Big things, little things, future things, past things, things that are, things that might be. Don't be anxious about *anything*.

In *every* situation, give thanks. Scary situations, hurtful situations, uncertain situations, disappointing situations. In *every* situation, give thanks.

When anxious thoughts surface and begin to multiply, what is the answer? Give thanks.

Sometimes distractions are the *other activities* we might have to forgo to choose time with the Lord. We might get distracted by checking email or social networking sites just before we sit down for focused prayer. One thing leads to another, and we find ourselves clicking on the next link or reading just one more post. Before we know it our planned prayertime is forgotten. The answer to that distractions is pretty simple: Have a rule. First things first. Be like a horse with blinders on. Straight to your sacred space, no detours.

I have always found it helpful to set up my sacred space before I go to bed. Clear it of clutter, gather my tools. In doing this, I am setting my mind that this is where I will be first in the morning. I find something about that ritual to set a sense of anticipation and expectation.

You might even become distracted during your prayertime by the *pull of other things you enjoy* and look forward to doing. Just acknowledge that the anticipation of a pleasurable activity is pulling at you, commit it to the Lord, discipline your mind back into the moment, and continue with your prayertime. You may have to do that several times in a single prayertime, but that's OK. Just do it. Maybe pray something like this: "Father, I choose You over everything else."

I suggest that whatever amount of time you have committed for your prayertime, you always stay to the last minute. Try not to think, *Well, I'm through early. I'll just go on my way.* Just as a discipline and a firm commitment, stay. You might feel restless. It might not feel very spiritual. But stay anyway. Do you think it's possible that the enemy might work to generate restlessness so that you will miss the richest time?

God keeps His word to you. He always does what He says He will do. Keep your word to Him. You have committed a certain portion of time to Him. Keep your word. When you choose by an act of your will to keep your word to Him, you are bringing offerings to Him. You are bringing the offering of your time and your attention. You are bringing your heart. You are incarnating your words of love to Him.

"I'm bringing my prizes and presents to your house. I'm doing what I said I'd do" (Psalm 66:13 The Message).

By its very nature, an offering costs you something. I love this illustration from the life of David. The Lord had commanded him to buy a threshing floor from a man named Araunah and build an altar there to offer sacrifices. Araunah wanted to give the threshing floor to King David, but David insisted on paying, with this explanation: "I will not sacrifice to the Lord my God burnt offerings that cost me nothing" (2 Samuel 24:24).

Offering your time and heart to the Lord will cost you something. That is part of what makes it an offering of love. But here is the irony: the value of what you receive is so overwhelmingly more than what it cost you that "cost" moves from the loss column into the gain column.

Several years ago, the news carried a human interest story. A woman bought an abstract painting from a junk store in California for $5. Ten years later, she discovered that the "junk" she purchased was likely an original Jackson Pollock painting and could be worth more than $10 million. Let's project our imaginations into the future and suppose that the woman has been paid $10 million for the painting that cost her $5. Let's imagine that she is sitting in the palatial mansion the money has afforded her and that she is dripping in jewels and draped in fine designer clothing, none of which she could have afforded previously. Imagine that I ask her, "What did that Jackson

Pollock painting cost you?" How do you think she would answer that question? I think she would say, "Cost me? It cost me nothing. It gained me $10 million and afforded me everything I own." When the profit far outweighs the investment, we call it gain. The initial cost is swallowed up in the benefit it obtains, and it shows up on the "profit" side of the balance sheet.

Count the cost, then count the reward.

GENERAL DISTRACTIONS

Sometimes we're just restless, predisposed to be unmindful of being present to the moment. Here are some ideas for combating this:

1. Use your body in worship. Kneel. Lift your hands. Use physical positions that mean something to you. If your body is not able to take those positions, or if it is more distracting to physically be in those positions, then mentally take positions of worship. In the inner sanctuary of your own soul, be in worship.

2. Many people find it helpful to write out their prayers to keep them focused. You could just write outlines or phrases if you are not given to writing prose.

3. Pray out loud.

4. Be physically away from distractions like computers, televisions, or phones. Have your phones turned off or silent.

5. Create the space for your prayertime with visual cues like pictures of loved ones for whom you pray.

6. Engage all your senses. Tabernacle worship as prescribed by God engaged all the senses. Set up your special location with things that are beautiful, fragrant, and melodious to you.

7. Read Scripture until something stops you—a phrase or word or idea jumps out at you. Stop there and pray out of that.

8. Read Scripture imaginatively. Put yourself into the character of a familiar story and watch the story unfold as if in real time. What do you see about who God is and who He promises to be for you? Pray out of that insight.

9. Use a scripturally sound devotional book.

10. Have someone in your life who is on a similar journey. Plan to share regularly—maybe weekly—how God is using your daily focused prayertimes. You can do this in person, by phone, by video chat, or any way that will be reasonable

and doable in your life. You will find yourself more attentive because you are going to share your experience or struggle.

11. Imagine Jesus in a chair in front of you. Some people even set up that chair. You are not making up things. Jesus is fully present right there with you. Find ways to keep His presence a reality for you. You are not praying to air. You are in a face-to-face conversation with the present Jesus.

JUST RETURN

When you find yourself distracted, just come on back. Don't berate yourself. God is the One who has brought your mind back to Him. He is like a magnet to your heart. He will always draw you back. Entrust yourself to Him.

REFRAME

Finding yourself distracted during times of prayer is a universal experience, but don't give into it. Use it. What most distracts you during times if prayer? Write it out.

REFOCUS

Acknowledge that you are distractible. Plan ahead for how you will deal with it. Work your plan.

CHALLENGE EIGHT

Feeling that prayer is having no effect and is wasted time

INVISIBLE DOES NOT MEAN IMPOTENT

Many times the key to powerful prayer is perseverance. Most of what Jesus spoke about prayer was encouragement to keep praying when it seems that nothing is happening. As you develop a deeper understanding of the dynamics of prayer, you will come to *know* what you cannot *see* (Hebrews 11:1). God is at work in response to prayer, whether you can see what He is doing or not. Prayer has its first effects in the spiritual realm. The spiritual realm is invisible, but not insubstantial. God's power is invisible, but invisible does not mean impotent.

It may be that what you can observe with your physical senses shows no change, but that does not mean things are not changing. You can be sure that God is faithful to respond to prayer and that prayer is moving His power and provision into the circumstances.

God has everything prepared and ready for you even before you need it. Prayer is what moves His provision from the spiritual realm and into the circumstances of earth. Prayer does not put God in motion. He has already moved and prepared. Prayer transports what He has prepared into your experience.

> *"'No eye has seen, no ear has heard, no mind*
> *has conceived what God has prepared for those*
> *who love him'—but God has revealed it to us by*

his Spirit. The Spirit searches all things, even the
deep things of God" (1 Corinthians 2:9–10).

God has everything you need prepared for you. Every answer to every need is ready and waiting. "And my God will meet all your needs according to his glorious riches in Christ Jesus" (Philippians 4:19). God has already said, "Yes." "No matter how many promises God has made, they are 'Yes' in Christ" (2 Corinthians 1:20). Everything you need for life or for godliness is freely available to you. Second Peter 1:3 assures you that "His divine power has given us everything we need for life [material needs] and godliness [spiritual needs] through our knowledge of him who called us by his own glory and excellence."

When you know that every need has already been prepared for, then you can experience the peace to which God calls you. You do not need to have anxiety about anything. Instead, you can trust Him for His provision. When you understand that God has everything prepared and waiting for you and that it comes into your life by means of prayer, then it makes sense to wrap your petitions in thanksgiving. "Do not be anxious about anything, but in everything, by prayer and petition, with thanksgiving, present your requests to God" (Philippians 4:6). You don't have to wait until you see the answer with your senses to know that you possess it. Even when you can't see what He's doing, you can know that He knew and prepared for your need even before you knew you had a need.

When I was a college student, I didn't pay my own bills. My dad paid them. When a bill would arrive at my post office box, although it was addressed to me and clearly stated that I owed a certain amount of money, I didn't feel the responsibility for it. I sent it on to my dad without even opening it. Once I dropped it in the mail to him, I never thought about it again. In my mind, it became his bill immediately. I never took ownership of the debt. I cast all my debts on him and left them there. Why? Because I knew that he had everything I needed available and he always released it on my behalf when I asked.

That's how it is with your heavenly Father. He is your provider. "Cast your cares on the Lord and he will sustain you" (Psalm 55:22). Once you bring God your request, consider that need met. Don't take possession of the need; instead, take possession of the supply. Your role is to take the need to your Father. Don't feel like the responsible party. You will have no reason to be anxious. Be expectant instead. The psalmist prays: "In the morning, Lord, you hear my voice; in the morning I lay my requests before you and wait expectantly" (Psalm 5:3). "He who promised is faithful, and he will do it" (1 Thessalonians 5:24). Don't wait until you see it to embrace it.

A NEW WAY OF SEEING

Prayer rarely produces instant change. It is not a cosmic vending machine—put in a prayer, get out an answer. Rather, it is a process. We often have a very narrow focus, but God is working according to a bigger agenda. If we try to narrow prayer down to our perspective, we will miss the work that God is doing. We often have our attention focused only on a specific outcome that we want to see, but God is working in a bigger arena to bring about a bigger result. In *Live a Praying Life*, I illustrate like this:

> For example, suppose that you said to me, "Will you pray that God will give me a car so that I can get to work?" My response to you would be, "I won't pray that God will give you a car, but I will pray that God will get you to work." Perhaps God wants to provide you with a ride with someone who will open the door for the next step in His plan. If your prayer focus is a car, but God provides for your need in another way, you will think that God has said no to your prayer. It will go in your "unanswered prayers" category.

Ask God to open the eyes of your heart so that you can perceive His work where you hadn't been looking for it earlier. Paul prays this:

> *"I keep asking that the God of our Lord Jesus Christ, the glorious Father, may give you the Spirit of wisdom and revelation, so that you may know him better. I pray that the eyes of*

your heart may be enlightened in order that you may know the hope to which he has called you, the riches of his glorious inheritance in his holy people, and his incomparably great power for us who believe." (Ephesians 1:17–19)

Paul knows that the ultimate goal of life is to "know him better." The word *know* here means to comprehend and understand. Since Paul wants people to understand God's heart, what does he ask? He asks that "the eyes of [their] heart may be enlightened."

In the physical realm, when light is present, your eyes are enabled to see what is in front of you. Apart from light, there is no vision. Paul implies that we have inner eyes and that they need to get light so they can "see." He suggests that when our inner eyes get light, then we can "see" what's right in front of us. The sentence says: "I pray that the eyes of your heart may be enlightened in order that you may *know*." This time the word *know* means to experience. He says that when our hearts have light, our inner eyes will be able to experience the reality of the spiritual realm. We will experience God's invisible power and His unseen activity and we will comprehend Him. Of course, not fully. Of course our minds can't grasp the full measure of God. But we can know what we need to know to navigate our circumstances in faith.

Now, look what comes next. When He gives light to those inner eyes, here is what you will experience that has been right in front of you.

1. "The hope to which he has called you." This hope is not just crossing your fingers and hoping for the best. Rather, it means a confident expectation. When He enlightens your inner eyes, you can see what you're hoping for. Your heart experiences that it is real. Not wishing, but expecting. His Word is where He will reveal the hope to which you can cling, the hope that anchors your soul no matter how choppy the sea. Be sure you are immersed in His Word.

2. "The riches of his glorious inheritance in his holy people." All of His great riches are to be used for your benefit. He holds nothing in reserve. His glorious riches are invested in His people. You don't have to look for His provision as if it is floating around on clouds somewhere in the far reaches of the cosmos. His riches are all invested. He has given us each other, and we are the repository of His great wealth. Be sure you are connected intimately with other believers.

3. "His incomparably great power for us who believe." His power that is so great it is incomprehensible. Paul, in the following verses, expounds on this power. He says that it is the very same power by which He raised Jesus from the dead and then lifted Him into the heavens to sit in power

at His right hand. That's the power you can experience. That's the power that is working everything out for your good right now. Not later, when you get the words right. Now. The Lord Himself will reveal this power to your heart, and you can believe it even before you see it. Be sure you are giving His Spirit plenty of room to do His work in you so that your spiritual vision will become sharper.

To recap, what your physical eyes can see and what you can observe with your senses does not tell the whole story. If you are trying to evaluate prayer's effectiveness based on earthly perceptions, then there is a whole dimension of activity that you are not taking into account.

PERSEVERE

Let me repeat: prayer rarely produces instant visible results. Part of the process of prayer is what happens in the period of time that elapses between your request and God's answer. During that time, realize two things. First, that God is at work on your behalf in your circumstances even when you can't see what He is doing. Charles H. Spurgeon said, "God is too good to be unkind. He is too wise to be confused. If I cannot trace His hand, I can always trust His heart."

Second, that waiting period is producing something of value. It is not wasted time or time when God is waiting for you to get prayer right. It is purposeful time, and God's purposes for you are always and only good. Let me share an illustration from *Heart's Cry*:

> Think about the incubation period during which a bird's fertilized egg reaches maturity and hatches a baby bird. Once a bird lays her eggs, she sits on them to incubate them. To the uninformed observer, it would appear that nothing is happening. That observer would be amazed if he knew just how much was happening. The incubating bird has tucked her eggs underneath her stomach feathers close to a bare spot called her incubation patch. The incubation patch is the warmest surface on the bird's body because of the network of blood vessels that lie close to the surface and produce heat. This heat is readily passed from the mother bird to her eggs. Her waiting is deliberate. The delay is essential to the outcome. All the work is invisible to the physical eye. As the mother sits on her eggs, the embryo is growing to a fully formed chick. When the chick is ready, it will hatch. Our persevering intercession provides the incubating heat needed for our Spirit-born desires to reach maturity.

Your prayers are effective from the moment you first begin to pray. You don't have to overcome any inertia on God's part to get things moving. Simultaneous with your first inarticulate sigh, heaven Is in motion. God doesn't take days off. Every single day of your waiting period has a function in what God is working out.

No need to be surprised that prayer is more than a once-and-done type activity. Jesus said it over and over.

In the praying life, God schedules waiting periods. The Word of God teaches that prayer—true prayer—is a long-term commitment. Jesus' teaching about prayer was, "Keep on asking and it will be given you; keep on seeking and you will find; keep on knocking . . . and the door will be opened to you" (Matthew 7:7 AMP). He teaches tenacity and perseverance. He told parables that illustrated persistent, persevering prayer. In one parable, He described a widow who came to an unjust judge over and over again until she received what she needed. Luke introduces this parable with these words: "Then Jesus told his disciples a parable to show them that they should always pray and not give up" (Luke 18:1). The whole point of Jesus' parable was to teach us not to give up. Why did Jesus think it necessary to teach such a thing? Because He knew that prayer would require the kind of steadfastness and resolve that could, if misunderstood, make a person give up. He taught us that when we feel like giving up, we must not give in to it. Prayer is not for quitters.

KEEP AT IT AND VICTORY IS YOURS

"Thanks be to God, who always leads us in triumphal procession in Christ and through us

spreads everywhere the fragrance of the knowl-edge of him. For we are to God the aroma of Christ among those who are being saved and those who are perishing. To the one we are the smell of death; to the other, the fragrance of life" (2 Corinthians 2:14–16).

"Thanks be to God, who *always* leads us in triumphal procession in Christ," Paul says. Paul is drawing on an image from the Roman culture. He creates a mental picture of a triumphal procession in which a triumphant Roman general is celebrated for his victorious campaign. The conquering general is preceded into the city by the captives taken in war and is followed by his triumphant troops. As the conquering troops paraded through the city, they shout, "Triumph!"

The Spirit of God, speaking through Paul, tells us that the triumphal procession in which we march is headed by Jesus, the Conqueror. He tells us that it is one continual triumphal march that began at the Cross and goes on endlessly into eternity. Paul uses the same imagery in Colossians 2:15: "And having disarmed the powers and authorities, he made a public spectacle of them, triumphing over them by the cross." Our enemies, whom the Scripture makes clear are the powers, principalities, and authorities of Satan's realm, are the army over whom Jesus has triumphed. (Read Ephesians 6:12.) The battleground on which the victory has been won is the Cross of Jesus. The conquering army is made up of believers—you and me. We are to be marching through life with the shout of "Triumph!" on our lips.

Even when what your eyes can see tells a story of discouragement, the reality is that you are part of the triumphal parade. You can go ahead and celebrate victory because it is sure. Align your thoughts with the truth. When anxiety knocks, refuse it entrance by expressing thanksgiving to God. When your requests are made with thanksgiving, His peace stands guard over your heart and mind.

BIG PICTURE

If your experience with prayer has been limited to trying to get God to perform for you when you need something, then you have missed out on what prayer is meant to be. If you are feeling that prayer is useless because you have prayed and prayed and not received what you were asking for, then I'm guessing that this might be your situation. I'm not saying this to scold you; I'm not trying to make you feel ashamed. In fact, I'm very excited for you. Here you are, reading this book. You're not satisfied with the experience so far, but you don't want to throw in the towel. Something keeps you at it. Actually, not *something*, but *Someone*. The Lord Himself won't let you go.

Once you learn to step back and see the bigger picture, your perspective will begin to change. There is a difference between appearance and reality. Apart from the Spirit, who enlightens the eyes of our hearts, we are limited to appearance and we miss the reality. Appearance is misleading. For example, based on appearance, one would conclude that the sun revolves around the earth. This has every appearance of being true, so an uninformed person would mistake it for truth. When the perception of truth is narrowly drawn, based on appearance, then all of our perceptions and emotions are guided by an illusion. When understanding does not correspond to reality, then a person is restricted and limited instead of being free.

I read a report from a group of scientists who were studying the rate at which the physical senses mature. They conducted an experiment in which crawling babies were being studied for depth perception. The babies were placed on a flat, level floor. The floor was a black-and-white checkerboard pattern. At a certain place in the floor, the checkerboard pattern changed. The alternating black-and-white squares became progressively smaller. This gave the visual illusion of a sudden steep drop-off. None of the babies would come near the place they perceived as the edge.

As I read this report, I thought, *How like us!* These babies were acting on their immature, uninformed perceptions of reality. Because they did not know about optical illusions, their activity was limited and restricted to a small area, when in reality they had a large space in which to safely play. If only they had known the truth, they would have been free to expand their horizons, but they are immature and cannot make judgments based on anything except appearance.

We, too, are inclined to feel safer if we base our actions and beliefs on what we can directly observe. We place great faith in the information our physical senses gather. We look at circumstances on the earth and mistake them for the full truth. We allow our earthbound perceptions to define our sense of reality. We limit ourselves by settling for what appears to be true. The babies' immature understanding caused them to restrict themselves.

In Plato's work, *The Republic*, we find a parable that well describes the difference between living by appearance and living by truth. I will condense it for you. It goes something like this:

Picture a race of men who live in an underground cave dwelling. This race of men has lived in this cave all their lives. Not only do they live underground, but their necks and legs are bound by chains in such a way that they cannot change positions or turn their heads. They are facing a cave wall, and it is all they have ever seen of the world. Some distance behind them, and higher up, a huge fire is burning. Between the fire and the chained men lives another race of men. This race moves and lives in such a way that the light from the fire casts their shadows on the cave wall.

The chained men only know the unchained men by the shadows cast on the cave wall. The acoustics in the cave cause it to seem that voices are coming from the shadows. The only truth they know is really shadow. They believe shadow to be substance because they have never seen the substance.

Imagine that one of these bound men one day breaks the chains, stands up, and begins to walk toward the light. His eyes, never having been exposed to light, first have to adjust to the light before he can see the objects that have been casting the shadows. He has a period of adjustment to the light, then begins to see substance for the first time. When he realizes that everything he knows and believes is really shadow, does he not consider himself blessed to be so enlightened? Does finding light and substance more than make up for the shadow existence he has left behind?

If I am going to define reality based on what I can observe with my senses, my entire existence will be defined by a misunderstanding. I will be limited and disoriented. I will believe shadow to be substance. If I look at the circumstances on earth and believe them to be the only solid reality, I will never know the fullness and completeness that Jesus offers.

Do you see why God wants us to know reality? Do you see that He longs for us to be free from the anxiety produced by perceptions that are not true? He does not want us to be held captive by conjecture and assumption. He wants us to be free to live abundantly. He wants to show us the rock-solid reality that underlies the appearance. When we keep our attention focused on circumstances—appearance—we will not see the big picture, and we will experience emotions based on a lie.

God is working out the big picture, but He is working it out in the details of life. He invites both macropraying (for big stuff) and micropraying (for smaller details). One of the ways that God teaches us that we can trust Him in the big things is to show us we can trust Him in the small things.

Jesus goes to great lengths to help us see how carefully we are cared for. He makes the point that God is in the very smallest details, so let that lead you to the conclusion that you can trust Him in the big events of life.

"Are not two sparrows sold for a penny? Yet not one of them will fall to the ground outside your Father's care. And even the very hairs of your head are all numbered. So don't be afraid; you are worth more than many sparrows" (Matthew 10:29–31).

"Look at the birds of the air; they do not sow or reap or store away in barns, and yet your heavenly Father feeds them. Are you not much more valuable than they? Can any one of you by worrying add a single hour to your life? And why do you worry about clothes? See how the flowers of the field grow. They do not labor or spin. Yet I tell you that not even Solomon in all his splendor was dressed like one of these. If that is how God clothes the grass of the field, which is here today and tomorrow is thrown into the fire, will he not much more clothe you—you of little faith?" (Matthew 6:26–30).

Jesus thinks it is important for His listeners to grasp this. God is at work on the micro level.

MICROPRAYING

Try an experiment. On purpose, give details of your day to God as they come up. This is my very grand prayer as I move through the details of my day: "Here, God." I'm not suggesting that you try to tell God how to smooth out your day or how to manage your life. Just, "Here, God." See what happens. He wants to show you Himself in the small, everyday details so that you will know you can trust Him in the big things. It's training ground. You are not monopolizing God's attention or distracting Him from more important things. He can do everything all the time at full power.

MACROPRAYING

While you're getting the hang of micropraying, learn about macropraying. While God has His fingerprints all over the details, the big things are taking shape. Nothing is too big a prayer. Nothing is too big a cause. Ask big. Then stand back and watch Him move. Slowly, maybe. Incrementally, probably. But move He will and the timing will be spot on.

REFRAME

Have you been discouraged about prayer's effect? Do you recognize that you may have been distracted from God's work by your small expectations? Write out your discouragement and what you are thinking about it now.

REFOCUS

Deliberately rethink your attitude and begin thanking God for all that He is doing that you don't yet see. Where you perhaps have been thinking, "I don't know why nothing is happening," change that to, "Thank You for everything that is happening."

CHALLENGE NINE

Feeling that you have to perform some kind of spiritual ritual to get God's attention before you can pray

JESUS IS SEEKING YOU OUT

God's attention never wanders from you. You have His full attention 24 hours of every single day. He keeps you as the apple of His eye (Psalm 17:8). That means that if you could look into His eyes, you would see your face reflected. He *keeps* you there—He never looks away.

When we pray, our prayer does not capture God's attention. We pray because God has captured our attention.

> It is not our prayer which moves the Lord Jesus. It is Jesus who moves us to pray.
>
> —OLE HALLESBY

God's love for us is a truth that sounds like a lie when first encountered. It makes no sense at all. Maybe He could tolerate us—but ardently, passionately love us? It boggles the mind. Yet it is affirmed from one end of Scripture to the other. It is what colors every word of Scripture.

His love for you began even before you were born. His careful attention to every detail of your life is rooted in His fathomless love.

> *For you created my inmost being; you knit me together in my mother's womb. I praise you*

because I am fearfully and wonderfully made;
your works are wonderful, I know that full well.
My frame was not hidden from you when I was
made in the secret place, when I was woven
together in the depths of the earth. Your eyes
saw my unformed body; all the days ordained
for me were written in your book before one of
them came to be. (Psalm 139:13–16)

Do you hear the love in those words? Do you hear Him telling you now that He has been actively loving you from before you were born? Every step you take, every challenge you encounter, every victory you win—all of it is under His watchful eye and His guiding hand. When you ponder how deeply you are loved, you will begin to really believe that you don't have to do anything at all to capture His attention.

LOVE THAT SOUGHT YOU OUT

Why would the Beloved become the Despised? Why would heaven's Darling become the lightning rod for heaven's wrath?

On that night in a stable in Bethlehem, from earth's view, a baby was born. From heaven's view, You, God the Son, voluntarily left Your rightful place on the universe's throne, left the riches and the unimaginable glory that were Your own possessions, left the sound of praise and worship that surrounded You day and night—left it all to be with us. What must that moment have been like? When heaven's great Treasure shed His kingly grandeur and donned mere clay, did the angels for a moment hold their breath and look on in astonishment? When He who was from the beginning took upon Himself the form of a servant, did the eternal realm halt—just for a heartbeat—and stand speechless with wonder? When the King of kings exchanged His majestic robes for swaddling clothes, surely it was the most beautiful, awe-inspiring moment in all eternity. . . . In the heavens, that which looked ordinary from the earth was the spark for unparalleled celebration (Hebrews 1:6). It was something never before seen and never to be seen again—when the King became a servant.

—*Pursuing the Christ: Prayers for Christmastime*

When you think about that momentous event, consider this. There was nothing in it for Him. He didn't get more glory. In fact, as He prayed on the night before His crucifixion, He prayed, "And now, Father, glorify me in your presence with the glory I had with you before the world began" (John 17:5). He didn't have more power. He didn't have more riches. What did He gain that made the Cross worth it? He gained you.

Hebrews 12:2 says, "For the joy set before him he endured the cross, scorning its shame, and sat down at the right hand of the throne of God." What was "the joy set before Him"? What was of such value to Him that He would endure the Cross and its shame? What was the prize He kept His eyes on? You and me! We were the prize He won.

In His position as God, He dwells in unapproachable light (1 Timothy 6:16). Unapproachable. We can't get to Him. Should we try we would be blinded and overpowered by His glory. To get even a glimmer of His presence, we would have to veil our faces. He took matters in hand. So that we would not have to veil our faces, He veiled His glory. He wrapped His glory in flesh and blood and stepped into the time and space constraints of earth. Why? To win the prize.

He prizes you. You are counted among His treasure (Malachi 3:17). He is proud of you, pleased with you. You don't have to do anything to move His heart in your direction. I think about when my children were born, and now as my grandchildren are being born—about the great love I have had for a newborn baby who has done nothing at all to deserve it or be worthy of it. All they do is exist, and I love them beyond description just because they are mine. That is just the shadow of what God is saying when He says, "You are Mine."

"Do not fear, for I have redeemed you; I have summoned you by name; you are mine" (Isaiah 43:1). You can put your name in this sentence and hear Him direct these words to you. *You are Mine.*

HIDE-AND-SEEK

Not only do you not have to get His attention, but you can't escape His attention. If you try your best to hide yourself from Him, He is a bloodhound on the scent. You are always in His sight and on His heart.

> *Where can I go from your Spirit? Where can I flee from your presence? If I go up to the heavens, you are there; if I make my bed in the depths, you are there. If I rise on the wings of the dawn, if I settle on the far side of the sea, even there your hand will guide me, your right hand will hold me fast. If I say, "Surely the darkness will hide me and the light become night around me," even the darkness will not be dark to you; the night will shine like the day, for darkness is as light to you. (Psalm 139:7–12)*

He will never give up on you. He will never throw up His hands and declare, "Never mind! Have it your way!" Because He loves you too much.

CHANGED BY LOVE

His love for you goes beyond an emotion He feels. His love for you informs His every action in your life. If you believe the unbelievable claim of His consuming love for you, you will find yourself being changed by the power of it.

In *What's So Amazing About Grace?*, Phillip Yancey writes, "Sociologists have a theory of the looking-glass self: you become what the most important person in your life (wife, father, boss, etc.) thinks you are. How would my life change if I truly believed the Bible's astounding words about God's love for me, if I looked in the mirror and saw what God sees?"

> *"And we all, who with unveiled faces contemplate the Lord's glory, are being transformed into his image with ever-increasing glory, which comes from the Lord, who is the Spirit"* (2 Corinthians 3:18).

In 2 Corinthians 3:18, Paul says that that we *contemplate*—a word that means to look for a long time, behold, and even reflect or see as in a mirror—the Lord's glory, His presence. Using the eyes of our hearts, we look into His face. Our faces are unveiled—nothing between us and Him. Face-to-face. When Paul is writing this, he is alluding to the way Moses used to meet with the Lord, and be changed by that encounter so profoundly that it showed on Moses's own face.

> "The Lord would speak to Moses face to face, as one speaks to a friend" (Exodus 33:11). When we read that statement it says something far beyond

the words in the sentence. Face-to-face. It implies intimacy. It suggests an open and revealing relationship. It means access. The presence of the Lord is His face to your face. It speaks of something beyond love. Beyond passion. It speaks of friendship. Real friendship. The kind of friendship where you can read one another's faces even without words. "I have sought your face with all my heart; be gracious to me according to your promise" (Psalm 119:58). "My heart says of you, 'Seek his face!' Your face, Lord, I will seek" (27:8). Seek His face. He invites you into His presence, to be before His face. . . . When Moses emerged from face time with the Lord, he was changed. The difference was so profound that it was reflected on his face. The skin on his face glowed so brightly that the change startled the Israelites. The effect of having been before the Lord's face was evident to observers. When we are face-to-face with the Lord, we are changed. We are changed in profound ways that are evident to those around us. His presence leaves no one unmarked. . . . We not only read each others' faces, we reflect them. Next time you're in deep conversation with someone, notice how the two of you begin to unconsciously reflect each other's facial expressions. Or watch two people who have had a long and intimate relationship. They make similar faces to express certain things.

—*Life Unhindered! Five Keys*
to Walking in Freedom

God has invited you to His face. Instead of you needing to find the ritual or the words and phrases that will garner His attention, you can know that He is forever focused on you. You can consider yourself His very favorite. Your being His favorite does not negate the fact that I am also His favorite, and each of His children is His favorite. Each of us has all of His attention all the time, as if He had only one of us to care for. Augustine said, "He loves each of us as if there were only one of us to love." C. S. Lewis puts it this way: "He has infinite attention to spare for each one of us. He does not have to deal with us in the mass. You are as much alone with Him as if you were the only being He had ever created. When Christ died, He died for you individually just as much as if you had been the only man in the world."

God is not carving up and divvying out His resources. He doesn't have to neglect one thing to deal with another. Jesus told many parables that emphasized the individual nature of His infinite and bottomless love. The shepherd who left his 99 sheep to search out the one lost sheep, for example (Matthew 18:12). One sheep mattered enough to get His full attention.

I love a story Mark tells about a woman who might have been lost in the crowd, except that Jesus saw her and singled her out from the throngs.

*A woman who had suffered a condition of hem-
orrhaging for twelve years—a long succession
of physicians had treated her, and treated her
badly, taking all her money and leaving her worse
off than before—had heard about Jesus. She
slipped in from behind and touched his robe. She
was thinking to herself, "If I can put a finger on his
robe, I can get well." The moment she did it, the
flow of blood dried up. She could feel the change
and knew her plague was over and done with.*

*At the same moment, Jesus felt energy dis-
charging from him. He turned around to the
crowd and asked, "Who touched my robe?"*

*His disciples said, "What are you talking
about? With this crowd pushing and jostling you,
you're asking, 'Who touched me?' Dozens have
touched you!"*

*But he went on asking, looking around to see
who had done it. The woman, knowing what had
happened, knowing she was the one, stepped
up in fear and trembling, knelt before him, and
gave him the whole story.*

*Jesus said to her, "Daughter, you took a risk
of faith, and now you're healed and whole. Live
well, live blessed! Be healed of your plague."*
(Mark 5:25–34 The Message)

Consider the setting. Jesus doesn't just have a big crowd around Him; he has a loud, raucous throng. All seeking for His attention. At this juncture He is on His way to the house of an important family to heal their ailing daughter. The woman in this story, due to her particular malady, was an outcast from her society and considered unclean and untouchable. After she had touched Jesus and received immediate healing, she had no intention of revealing herself to Him. She tried to hide. But Jesus' love compelled Him to stop everything else, even His progress toward the home of the important family, to seek a face-to-face encounter with an insignificant unclean woman who expected to be lost in a crowd. Even when she tried to stay off His radar screen, Jesus would not allow it.

Jesus is seeking you out, calling you to His face. He is determined that you will not miss what He has to offer you. Even if you try to keep Him at arm's length in your life, He will pursue your heart relentlessly.

Let prayer become a turning toward Him, seeking His face, seeing yourself in His eyes. Let it be the heart-to-heart flow of love that transforms you and frees you and fills you. Let His active, seeking love mold and shape you until prayer is as natural as breathing. Prayer is nothing more complicated than receiving love.

MULTILAYERED LOVE

His love is so deep and beyond our ability to fully grasp that He employs numerous images as description. Look at just a few and let the picture He paints help you "grasp how wide and long and high and deep is the love of Christ, and to know this love that surpasses knowledge" (Ephesians 3:18–19).

> Father
> *"There you saw how the L*ORD *your God carried you, as a father carries his son" (Deuteronomy 1:31).*

> Mother
> *"Can a mother forget the baby at her breast and have no compassion on the child she has borne? Though she may forget, I will not forget you!" (Isaiah 49:15).*

> Shepherd
> *"He tends his flock like a shepherd: He gathers the lambs in his arms and carries them close to his heart; he gently leads those that have young" (Isaiah 40:11).*

In each of these descriptions, His love is the pursuing love. His love is the tender, watchful, protective, nourishing love. The object of His love does not have to win it or deserve it. He tells us over and over that we can rest in His love for us.

REFRAME

Have you been trying hard to get God's attention? Is there anything you do because you fear that if you don't do it, God will not hear you? Write out how you see God's unwavering love toward you.

REFOCUS

Be deliberate in thinking on God's love for you. Pick out one image and think on it and bask in it all day, then pick another image, and another. God went to great lengths to give images of His love for you. Cling to them.

CHALLENGE TEN

Feeling so bruised and broken that you don't have the will to participate in anything that requires engagement

HE ALONE IS YOUR RESCUER

May I first say, I know how you feel. I know how it feels to be in such deep grief that you don't have the emotional energy to reach out, and the idea of time spent in quiet reflection would just be time spent in the throes of wretched grief. I know.

During my time of dark grief after my husband's death, instead of feeling drawn to quiet time alone with the Lord, I avoided it. I knew that I was in continual interaction with Him, but I avoided the times of intimacy and listening because I felt I would have nothing to distract me from my heartache. Then the Lord spoke to me from this verse. "A bruised reed he will not break, and a smoldering wick he will not snuff out" (Isaiah 42:3). I remembered the tenderness of God and how kind and solicitous He is toward us. If I would just return to my commitment to daily focused time heart-to-heart with Him, maybe I would find comfort in the quiet. If I would change my mind and seek His presence, I would find the truth of His promise that "in quietness and trust is your strength" (30:15).

A BRUISED REED

Such a rich visual—a reed. Not a branch or a stem, but a reed. Flimsy. Weak. Breakable. Vulnerable to every puff of wind or pelt of rain or careless passerby. At risk of being crushed or trampled.

The reed is bruised. Here the Hebrew word for "bruised" means more than a surface wound. "Just a bruise," we say. This is more than that. It means the kind of deep inner crushing that might produce internal organ damage or internal bleeding. Something that might leave you looking whole on the outside but dying on the inside.

Now let's put our Savior into the picture. He takes up the cause of the fragile, vulnerable reed. What would He have to do to keep that bruised reed from breaking? I think He has to station Himself between the reed and the wind and rain. He has to make Himself a canopy over it. He has to surround it with Himself. Nothing gets to the reed without encountering Him.

Gentle Jesus—gentle toward the reed, but fierce toward the elements that would break it. His presence deflects all danger while the reed heals and regains its strength. In the shelter of Jesus, the reed can find relief.

A SMOLDERING WICK

A smoldering wick—the fire nearly out. Just a spark remains. Weak. Wavering. Assailable. Exposed. The slightest breath would snuff it out. At full strength, fire is strong and determined and a force to be reckoned with, but here it is barely alive. This small, barely there spark is latent and passive.

Now let's put our Savior into the picture. He comes to the rescue of the smoldering wick. He sees the little spark that has almost disappeared. He sees it and He loves it and He determines that it will not be snuffed out. He will guard it until it flames up again. What does He need to do to protect the smoldering wick? He cups His hands around it, shielding it from wind or breath. His big hands form a shield around it through which that last gust—the gust that will quench it all together—cannot pass.

Sweet Jesus. Devoted to His task. Surrounding the smoldering wick with His nail-scarred hands until life is restored.

THE COMFORT OF HIS PRESENCE

I found in those days of deep pain that the times of focused prayer were different. For a while, they were pretty focused on me and my pain. I experienced those times as healing balm being lovingly applied to my sad, beaten up heart. I didn't try to participate, I just sat. I entertained my self-absorbed sadness, but I did it aware of His presence. Little by little—very slowly—I began to have enough strength to reach toward Him as He had never stopped reaching toward me. When I couldn't hold on to Him, He held on to me.

Imagine that you are a parent with a recalcitrant toddler in tow and you need to cross a street with heavy traffic. You hold your toddler's hand. If he squirms and resists and tries to break free of you grip, will you let go? Or will you hold all the tighter?

Looking back from the vantage point of a few years, I see how tightly He held on to me while I tried to wiggle out of His grasp. Stubborn love held me and brought me safely through.

Have I described anything like what you are going through? Could I encourage you today to take the little step of giving Him the opening into your heart that will give you the environment in which you can heal? Baby steps. Small commitments. No expectations or demands, just poured out love.

YOUR HOPE

"Yes, my soul, find rest in God; my hope comes from him. Truly he is my rock and my salvation; he is my fortress, I will not be shaken" (Psalm 62:5-6).

Only in God will my heart find rest and peace. God is not the burden giver. He is the burden bearer. If you are carrying a soul burden, God wants to lift it from you. He wants you to find rest and relief from burdens you were never meant to carry. He is your soul's home. Anywhere but in Him, you are an outsider. You will find soul rest in God alone.

Your hope comes only from Him. He is the only source of everything that your soul hopes and longs for. The hope that

God offers is not like hope the world offers. Earthly hope is wishful thinking. God hope is confident, sure expectation. The word *hope* (*tigvah* in Hebrew) literally means "a cord." It comes from a primary root word, meaning "entwining."

Picture the hope God offers you like this: you have fallen into a deep ravine. As you look around, you see no means of escape. The ravine is so deep that no one will hear you if you cry for help. The walls are so steep and so treacherous that climbing is out of the question. You are in a hopeless situation from which you cannot rescue yourself. Suddenly you look up and see a person at the top of the ravine. What kind of hope does that inspire in you? It can only inspire wishful thinking. Hope is shadowy and insubstantial. "If only there were some way for that person to reach me, I would be saved."

You notice that the person has a rope. Hope has a little more substance. "If that rope is long enough to reach me and strong enough to hold me, I could be saved."

Your rescuer throws down the rope. It is long enough. It is strong enough. You wrap it securely around yourself and grab hold of it with your hands. Hope has a more solid basis. "If that person is strong enough to pull me up, I will be saved."

You recognize your rescuer. He is the strongest person who has ever lived. His exploits are legendary. Pulling your weight won't even tax his strength. This will be easy for Him. Hope becomes confidence. "I will be saved."

Now you have God hope. As long as you cling to that rope, you are being pulled out of the ravine by the strongest person who ever lived. At times, the pace may be slow. At times, the path may be difficult, but you are bound to your rescuer by a strong rope, which is entwined around you. Your hope comes from Him.

Isn't that a wonderful picture? You are bound to God by a cord called hope. Because of who He is, you have the confident, sure expectation that He will save you from any situation.

YOUR ROCK AND YOUR SALVATION

He alone is your rock. He alone is solid ground for your feet. He alone is sure and immovable. Charles H. Spurgeon said, "They trust God not *at all* who trust him not *alone*. He that stands with one foot on a rock, and another foot upon a quicksand, will sink and perish, as certainly as he that standeth with both feet upon a quicksand."

He alone is your salvation. He alone is your rescuer. The word *salvation* is from a Hebrew root word meaning "open, wide, or to free" (*yasha* in Hebrew). Eugene Peterson translates the word *salvation* in this Psalm "breathing room for my soul" (*The Message*). He is the One who saves you, sets you free, and gives you room to breathe.

YOUR FORTRESS

He alone is your fortress. He alone is the protector from all your enemies. He is your security and your safety. He is your hiding place from danger. "You are my hiding place; you will protect me from trouble and surround me with songs of deliverance" (Psalm 32:7).

When I was a little girl, when darkness fell, I was certain that terrible monsters were lurking in my room, just waiting to eat me up. As my fear grew, I would finally be motivated to make the mad dash from my monster-infested room to my parents' room. I would jump into their bed and lie right between them. Here I felt perfectly safe. Here I was fearless. I still thought the monsters were around. I just knew that they couldn't get to me in my safe position between my parents. When I was safely in my parents' bed, I could sleep peacefully in spite of the monsters. I knew that no monsters could get past them. They were my fortress.

You will not be shaken. Hidden in Him, surrounded by Him, protected by Him you will never be dislodged from your firm footing. He is "an impregnable castle" (*The Message*).

SLOW STEADY PROGRESS

God rarely works fast as we define "fast." However, He is always working. He is careful and deliberate. He is not in a hurry. He accomplishes each step of His process perfectly and completely, and everything He does is building toward His finale. Your pain won't disappear magically when you begin to turn to Him for healing. But the work will be sure and deep and rooted.

This is what the kingdom of God is like. A man scatters seed on the ground. Night and day, whether he sleeps or gets up, the seed sprouts and grows, though he does not know how. All by itself the soil produces grain—first the stalk, then the head, then the full kernel in the head. As soon as the grain is ripe, he puts the sickle to it, because the harvest has come. (Mark 4:26–29)

Nothing springs forth full-grown. Everything in the material creation and everything in the spiritual realm is progressively revealed. For this reason, it requires both faith and patience to see the fullness of God's work in your life. "We do not want you to become lazy, but to imitate those who through faith and patience inherit what has been promised. . . . And so after waiting patiently, Abraham received what was promised" (Hebrews 6:12, 15).

Faith is the ability to know for certain what you cannot observe with your physical senses. (See Hebrews 11:1.) The word translated "patience" suggests a tranquil soul, a sedate mind, an unruffled attitude toward difficulty, a steadiness of purpose.

God promised Abraham specifically: "I will surely bless you and give you many descendants" (6:14). Yet this promise was progressively unfolded. God did not make the promise and fulfill the promise on the same day. A long period of time elapsed between the promise and its fulfillment. Abraham had to exercise faith and patience before the fulfillment of the promise entered his experience.

Abraham's faith journey was much like the farmer's experience in Jesus' parable. When the seed was planted—when Abram received God's promise—a long period ensued that appeared from the earthly perspective to be desultory. Weeks, months, years, decades passed with no sign of the promised heir. God was working. We see it clearly in retrospect. But His work was underground; His work was invisible to the physical eye. Yet that period of invisible activity was bringing about exactly the right setting, exactly the right time, and exactly the right heart to put the promise on the earth at the opportune moment. When that moment arrived—that exactly right predetermined moment—the stalk appeared—Isaac was born. Then the head appeared—the nation of Israel grew more numerous than the sands on the seashore or the stars in the sky. Then the full kernel in the head—the Messiah was born and brought salvation and redemption.

God's promises will still enter our lives in the same way that God's promise to Abraham entered his life. First the seed, then the waiting and training period during which we exercise faith and patience, then the stalk, the head, and finally, the full kernel in the head. This is God's pattern and He never deviates from it. He never acts like a vending machine or an instant scratch-and-win game. His purpose is too far-reaching, His plans are too long-term, His riches are too precious for Him to throw them at us like confetti. He must prepare the ground in which the promise will grow. As the fulfilled promises appear in our experience, they are well-rooted and fully nourished because of the faith and patience that has fertilized them.

When the farmer plants the seed, the harvest is a forgone conclusion. When God's specific promises come into your life, the fulfillment is a forgone conclusion. It is impossible for Him to lie. The farmer could miss the harvest only one way: by leaving his field behind. He might grow impatient with the process and decide that the seed would not really produce the plant. He might imagine that he could get a quicker harvest somewhere else. He might decide that it's easier to buy someone else's harvest instead of waiting on his own. The harvest would still come, but he would not be there to put the sickle to it.

This time of unobservable work, this time during which the seed is germinating, is a time of activity and a time in which God's power is operating mightily. We will only know this work by faith because faith is what connects our earthly minds to spiritual reality. Don't mistake the appearance of inactivity for God's delay. He is not delaying; He is working in the invisible realm.

He promises to heal your heart. Though you might not feel it yet, He is at work in you and for you.

> *"The Lord is close to the brokenhearted and saves those who are crushed in spirit. The righteous person may have many troubles, but the Lord delivers him from them all"* (Psalm 34:18–19).

"He heals the brokenhearted and binds up their wounds" (Psalm 147:3).

"The Spirit of the Sovereign Lord is on me, because the LORD has anointed me to proclaim good news to the poor. He has sent me to bind up the brokenhearted, to proclaim freedom for the captives and release from darkness for the prisoners, to proclaim the year of the LORD's favor and the day of vengeance of our God, to comfort all who mourn, and provide for those who grieve in Zion—to bestow on them a crown of beauty instead of ashes, the oil of joy instead of mourning. (Isaiah 61:1–3)

Isaiah 61:1–3 is a description of the Messiah's role. Jesus claimed this very passage as referring to Himself. He deliberately read it in the Synagogue: "The scroll of the prophet Isaiah was handed to him. Unrolling it, he found the place where it is written" (Luke 4:17). He deliberately looked for just this passage to read. Having read it, "Then he rolled up the scroll, gave it back to the attendant and sat down. The eyes of everyone in the synagogue were fastened on him. He began by saying to them, 'Today this scripture is fulfilled in your hearing'" (Luke 4:20–21).

He publicly claimed this job description to be His. Notice how much of it has to do with healing broken hearts and comforting those who mourn and grieve. You will not grieve forever. Grief ends. He promises to "bestow on them a crown of beauty instead of ashes, the oil of joy instead of mourning."

YOU ARE WEAK, BUT HE IS STRONG

It's OK that you are weak. Stop trying to work up strength and let Him strengthen you. Think of a mighty elixir—a cure-all mixture full of life and healing and hope and salvation—being transfused into your heart like restorative medications can be transfused into your body. Just lay back and take it in. Be still and know that He is God. He's got this.

REFRAME

Accept that you are in a season of weakness, and don't try to pretend otherwise. Being weak doesn't make you bad. If your once fiery faith has become a smoldering wick, let His strong hands protect you. If you look fine on the outside, but you're dying on the inside, let His presence be a canopy over you. Write out how you are feeling right now.

REFOCUS

Determine that you will turn your pain toward God instead of avoiding time alone with Him and turning to other distractions for relief. The short-lived relief of outside distractions is not healing you. Let your daily times of focused prayer be times when you nurture the awareness of His healing, protective love.

CONCLUSION

I hope that you have encountered the Lord Himself as you were reading this book. I pray that the words on the pages are the words from His heart to yours. I hope you have found encouragement and that the principles here are freeing to you, not guilt-inducing.

> "The LORD confides in those who fear him, he makes known his covenant to them" (Psalm 25:14).

The Lord wants to bring you into His inner circle where He reveals His secrets to those whose heart is ever turned toward Him. Accept the invitation.

I am so passionate about prayer that I often explain that prayer is my obsession. I have thought about it, practiced it, wrestled with it for decades. It is a well that never runs dry. I want you to be excited about prayer.

In this book, I have touched on topics and ideas that I have written about in great depth and detail in other works. If your interest was piqued about prayer and you want to learn in more depth, I suggest *Live a Praying Life: Open Your Life to God's Power and Provision* as a starting place. This book is what I consider to be my reason for being born. It is the compilation of years of digging deep and being before the Lord with all my questions.

Visit prayinglife.org to find resources and free materials ready for download.

Thank you for spending some of your time with me in *Prayer Fatigue*. May the Lord's blessings overflow in your life.

New Hope® Publishers is a division of WMU®, an international organization that challenges Christian believers to understand and be radically involved in God's mission. For more information about WMU, go to wmu.com. More information about New Hope books may be found at NewHopeDigital.com. New Hope books may be purchased at your local bookstore.

Use the QR reader on your
smartphone to visit us online at
NewHopeDigital.com

If you've been blessed by this book, we would like to hear your story. The publisher and author welcome your comments and suggestions at: newhopereader@wmu.org.

Other Resources on Prayer by national best-selling author

JENNIFER KENNEDY DEAN

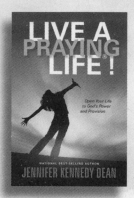
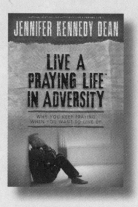
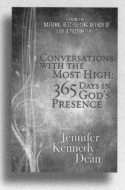